A Book of Bryn Mawr Stories

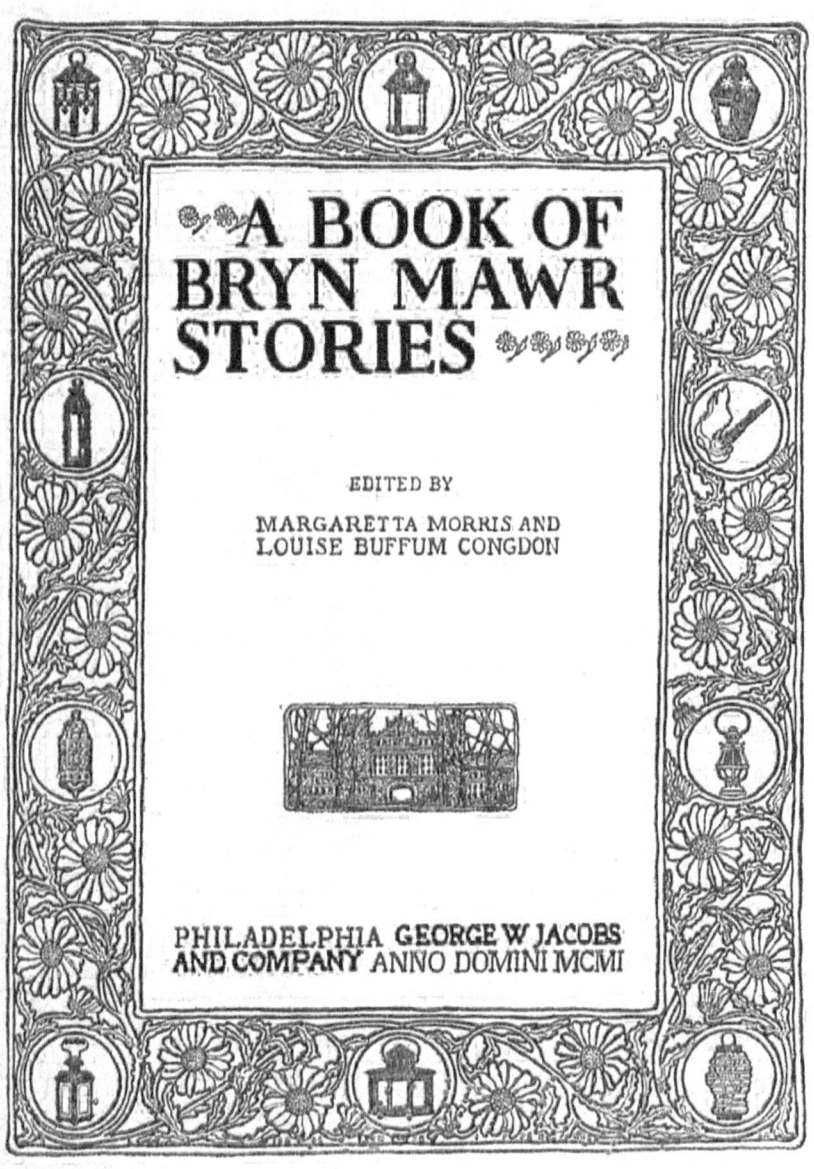

A BOOK OF BRYN MAWR STORIES

EDITED BY

MARGARETTA MORRIS AND
LOUISE BUFFUM CONGDON

PHILADELPHIA GEORGE W JACOBS
AND COMPANY ANNO DOMINI MCMI

Annotated Edition
Foreword and Notes by Mark E. Koltko-Rivera
New York City • The Bi-Co Press • 2014

A Book of Bryn Mawr Stories: Annotated Edition
edited by Margaretta Morris and Louise Buffum Congdon,
with foreword and notes by Mark E. Koltko-Rivera;
reprint edition published December 2013 by The Bi-Co Press,
an imprint of LVX Publications, New York City.

The first edition of this book was published in 1901 by George W. Jacobs & Co., which held the copyright at that time.

ISBN-13: 978-0-6159-3159-3   ISBN-10: 0-6159-3159-6
Copies sold in the U.S. are printed in the United States of America.

The contents of this book do not necessarily represent the policies or views of either the publisher or Bryn Mawr College. This book is not sponsored, sanctioned, or approved by Bryn Mawr College.

Front cover: photograph of M. Carey Thomas (detail); undated photograph of Pembroke Hall, Bryn Mawr College.

www.MarkKoltko-Rivera.com   authorMEKR@yahoo.com

Copies of this book may be purchased online at:
   http://astore.amazon.com/marswri-20

Booksellers: Check with your distributor for this book.

The Bi-Co Press publishes books by and for the alumnae, alumni, current students, and past and present faculty of the Bi-College Community, composed of Bryn Mawr and Haverford Colleges.

This Annotated Edition
is dedicated to
the members of the
Bryn Mawr College
Classes of 1975-1981.

Ad multos annos.

Contents

Foreword (2013)

A Book of Bryn Mawr Stories, a collection of short stories written by alumnae and then-current students of Bryn Mawr College about student life in that environment, was originally published in 1901. The present book is not a photographic reproduction, but a reprint edition, with new pagination, fresh type, and many footnotes (given that not every college student over the last fifty years has taken Latin, or read the poetry of the English Decadents). All footnotes in this book are my own, hence none are bracketed. The authors's original (often British) spelling and punctuation have been preserved.

Of the editors and authors of these stories, we may infer a great deal. That they were highly intelligent and talented is clear from the stories themselves, which mix witty (and occasionally multilingual) repartee with serious consideration of weighty ideas. The measure of the editors's determination is seen in the fact that they managed to get their anthology of short stories by unknown writers published by a major regional publisher.

For that is what George W. Jacobs & Co. was becoming, in 1901. Actively publishing in Philadelphia at least as early as 1899, and at least as late as 1925, Geo. Jacobs & Co. would bring forth a major work by Jacob Riis in 1903, and the first edition of Booker T. Washington's biography of Frederick Douglass in 1906.

It is in Geo. Jacobs & Co.'s publication record that I find yet another indication of distinction for the editors of *A Book of Bryn Mawr Stories*. Working from online listings of antiquarian booksellers (Bibliopolis and AbeBooks), I was able to identify 32 separate titles published by Geo. Jacobs & Co. (including the present one) for which the gender of the author/s or editor/s could be determined with a reasonable degree of certainty. Of those, only 8 (or 25%) had at least one female author or editor. It is not by chance that Bryn Mawr alumnae would show up in that short list.

Reading the editors's preface and the stories, one does note how the Bryn Mawr of a century ago is different from that of our own era, in matters of substance, style, and mindset. For example, a contemporary collection of Bryn Mawr stories would probably not make reference to "Bryn Mawr *girls*" except in irony. In addition, Bryn Mawr in 1901 emphasized classical languages and mathematics much more than the liberal arts; the social sciences practically did not exist in most American colleges at that time, and they did not exist at Bryn Mawr.

There is little in the way of overt racial, ethnic, sexual, or gender diversity among the students at the Bryn Mawr of these stories (as was the case in most of American higher education in that era). When a student in one of these stories talks about "coming out," she is discussing a débutante ball or cotillion.

This is a College well before the era of the special relationship between Bryn Mawr, Haverford, and Swarthmore. Even physically, this was a different world; indeed, this is a Bryn Mawr without a Rockefeller Hall (which would not be completed until 1904), or even a Thomas Library (1907), let alone a Goodhart Hall (1928) or a Rhoads Hall (1939).

And yet, so much here is familiar, well over a century after publication. We see this in the depiction of the College's educational values, its traditions, the experience of college life, and the characterization of its students.

Bryn Mawr was quite young when this book first appeared, the college having been founded in 1885, a mere 16 years before the book's publication. These stories are set firmly within the Bryn Mawr of M. Carey Thomas, who had been appointed Dean of the College in 1884, and then elected second president of the College in 1894 at the age of 37. (Thomas would remain as Dean until 1908, and as President of Bryn Mawr College until 1922, a generation after the last of the authors of the stories here had graduated.) Thomas was determined to challenge women intellectually, and to demonstrate to the world that women were intellectually at least the equals of men, and the effect on the authors of these stories is striking: the Bryn Mawr characters in these stories are simply the brightest, smartest, most intellectually sophisticated of any females in the fiction of the period, so far as I am aware. They are not only stunningly brilliant, but socially engaged in the issues of their time, particularly concerning women's education and the role of women in the contemporary world.

Certainly all of this accords with the reality of the Bryn Mawr that I knew in the late 1970s. To judge from the alumni publications that I have been reading for over 35 years now, the characterization above reflects the reality of the College's students today.[1]

Among the things upon which M. Carey Thomas left her stamp at the College were its traditions, informed by the classical and medieval world that she knew so well. (One might recall that Thomas's doctoral dissertation at the University of Zurich was a celebrated philological analysis of *Sir Gawain and the Green Knight*.) We read of some of those traditions in these stories: May Day, of course, and seniors singing on the steps of Taylor Hall. Although class lanterns are not mentioned explicitly, their existence is clearly implied by the title of the publication *The Lantern*, and by the illustration of a class-type lantern in the original title page, reproduced on the title page herein.

Some of the school songs are different, as I mention in the footnotes—but there *are* songs in these stories's Bryn Mawr, songs which, it would appear, are known by all the students, some of whom burst into renditions without warning. This is true to the Bryn Mawr that I knew in the late Seventies, and I daresay it is likely true today.

And, of course, there are the places that defined Bryn Mawr, then and now. In addition to the aforementioned Taylor Hall, Dalton, Denbigh, Merion, and Radnor all appear in these stories, along with Pembroke and its famous arch.

The greatest resonance for me in these stories lies in the depictions of student life. For example, consider this passage, from Harriet Jean Crawford's story "Catherine's Career"—noting that, in the era of the story, first semester final exams fell after the winter holiday break, and hence were known as "mid-years":

> With mid-years, a twenty-four page essay, Latin and
> English private reading and all sorts of unfinished odds

---

[1] During the period I was composing this Foreword, I happened to read the newly issued November 2013 edition of the *Bryn Mawr Alumnae Bulletin*. One article described how seven students in a French class are helping oppressed women in the Democratic Republic of Congo bring their experiences to the English-speaking world. Another described how a 2013 graduate of the College was using her Fulbright year to interpret the experience of young Athenians in the current Greek economic crisis, using a framework built on existentialism and the philosophy of the absurd. I could go on, but I trust that my point is made. Bryn Mawr did not have a monopoly on female brilliance in 1901, but it had and has still an astonishingly effective development enterprise for that commodity.

and ends of labour, one's previous misfortunes vanish
behind the rapidly accumulating wretchedness of the
four weeks after the Christmas vacation. This is the period at Bryn Mawr when one wonders what on earth
became of the first part of the semester, and one firmly
resolves this time at least to keep good resolutions and
never again be guilty of such improvident idleness; this
is the period when one wakes up on bright, crisp
mornings to the wretched realization that an examination is due next day in a subject of which one knows or
feels that one knows absolutely nothing; this is the period when, after struggles too painful to describe, one
turns up on the fatal morning pallid but resolute,
armed with a pen and scraggy blotter and with Tennyson's immortal words "theirs but to do or die," ringing
in one's ears; this is the period when after seizing the
examination questions one thrills or congeals in proportion to the number of intimate friends, bowing acquaintances or total strangers there enrolled.

How much of this would be different at the College today? I
would guess not much (aside from the lack of blotters). If not Latin or
Greek, perhaps it is archaeology, organic chemistry, Hebrew, or psychology that kicks the sugar plums out of the dreams of today's
Mawrter during first semester examinations. Similarly, one reads here
of changes in religious commitments during one's college years, of
feminism (as it existed a generation before national suffrage for wom-
en became a reality), of reflections provoked by study abroad—all of
these being lively concerns for many Bryn Mawr students today.

Another aspect of this collection that is very revealing, if rather
subtle, is the involvement of so many alumnae in the authorship of
these stories. This was the editors's design, of course. But it must be
noted that the editors reported no difficulty in gathering stories from
Bryn Mawr alumnae. Five of the stories, or half the collection, were
written by alumnae who had graduated four or more years before this
book originally was published. In our own era, it is sometimes hard
for those outside the Bi- (or Tri-) College Community to understand
that a large proportion of Bryn Mawr alumnae remain strongly at-

tached to their school, often enough, for life. Apparently this strength of attachment goes back a very long time, to judge by the alumnae presence in this collection.

The intellectual and social engagement, the ambition and achievement, the sheer cerebral horsepower that one sees exhibited by the students of these stories[2]—even the precision of their malediction[3]—all this resonates with my own experience of Mawrters, three quarters of a century after the stories that appear here were written. And I find myself, like Cora Armistead Hardy's character Charlotte, sighing and saying, "I wish I were a freshman again"—largely because I spent entirely more time at Bryn Mawr during my freshman year than was prudent, although it was wise. As a Haverford student myself (and I wear the sweatshirt as I type these words), I lived for three years in Bryn Mawr's Rhoads Hall (in the official dormitory exchange, thank you). That was not an accident. Reading these stories reminded me of why this happened.

It also made me eager to see the alumnae of my era, or more recent years, write their own books of Bryn Mawr stories.

Mark E. Koltko-Rivera, Ph.D.
Haverford College Class of 1978
December 12, 2013
New York City

www.MarkKoltko-Rivera.com; e-mail: authorMEKR@yahoo.com

Dr. Koltko-Rivera is a Fellow of the American Psychological Association. His scholarship has won awards from the Society for Humanistic Psychology, the Society for the Psychology of Religion and Spirituality, and the Society for General Psychology.

---

[2]   The students in Georgiana Goddard King's "Free Among the Dead" are discussing Nietzsche's *Übermensch* barely five years after *Thus Spoke Zarathustra* first appeared in English translation. This is a very sharp crew.

[3]   Some personal favorites: in Marian T. MacIntosh's "Her Masterpiece" we read "You piece of absurdity"; in Ellen Rose Giles's "The Apostasy of Anita Fiske" we note "Come, you lazy object." Another, from Edith Campbell Crane's "A Diplomatic Crusade": "Eleanor, leaning over and spanning Marjorie's forehead with her hand, murmured 'Undue cerebral enlargement——.'"

Preface (1901)

In compiling a volume of Bryn Mawr stories, the editors have been conscious that such a book could never adequately represent the college life. Its strong subtle character that commands the devotion of every Bryn Mawr student is something difficult if not impossible to depict. Yet there comes a time in the life of a college, as of an individual, when self-expression is inevitable. Such a time, the editors believe, has come for Bryn Mawr. And this conviction has induced them to bring out the present volume.

Until now the literary efforts of the students have concerned themselves with external matters rather than with introspection. Perhaps this is due to an instinctive reticence we Bryn Mawrtyrs have wherever our feelings are deeply stirred. We can joke about ourselves and our traditions as we do in *The Fortnightly Philistine*. But when we come to speak seriously to the outside world, as in *The Lantern*, we confine ourselves for the most part to subjects of general literary interest, practically ignoring the college atmosphere. At last, however, the ice is broken, and Bryn Mawr talks about herself.

In the earliest days, when the college had only two buildings and forty-four students, even in that first year it had a character and a spirit all its own. And fifteen years of rapid growth have seemed but to strengthen its individuality. To show the college unity in diversity the editors have carefully chosen authors from the older and younger alumnæ and from the undergraduates. They hope that in this way a truer impression of the college life may be given than would be possible if the whole book were written by one person.

Some readers may ask which of the many heroines in these tales is the typical Bryn Mawr girl. The reply is no one, but all. Bryn Mawr students come from all parts of the country, from all sorts of different surroundings, and on entering college they do not, popular prejudice to the contrary, immediately drop their individuality and become samples of a type. We have among our number the pedant, the coquette, the athlete, the snob, the poser, the girl who loves dress and prettiness, and she who affects mannish simplicity, the all-round girl, the serious-minded, and the frivolous. Yet none of these is the Bryn

Mawr girl *par excellence.* That mythical personage can be known only by comparing and contrasting her various incarnations.

This book is an attempt to show some of her incarnations and some typical scenes of Bryn Mawr life. College life is not dramatic and college stories have no great dramatic interest, unless they introduce elements foreign to the campus. Those who look to these stories, therefore, for entertainment may be disappointed, since most of them are serious in tone, and in their appeal to the reader depend largely upon the charm of local colour.

If in the mind of any one the spirit portrayed in this book is unworthy, if it falls short of the ideal of what college life should be, let it be remembered that this is a first attempt, and let the expression be blamed but not the Bryn Mawr spirit.

All of the following stories are new, and were written for this book, except *Studies in College Colour,* which are reprinted from *The Lantern* of 1893. One of these studies, the description of Chapel, has appeared also in *Cap and Gown in Prose.* For permission to use this last the editors are indebted to the courtesy of Messrs. L. C. Page & Company.

M. M. 1900.
L. B. C. 1900.

A Book of Bryn Mawr Stories

HER MASTERPIECE

I

For the first time in many years Ellen Blake was conscious of inability. Of course she could not have expected that her good fortune
would last forever. And yet, it must be confessed, that her helplessness
coming, as it did, when she had every reason to feel confident, had
been altogether a surprise, had, indeed, taken her at a cruel disad-
vantage. She was the more disconcerted at finding herself unable to do
what she had promised when she thought of the serious responsibility
resting upon her. It was wholly natural that she should be looking at
the predicament with the eye not of an ordinary being but of a personage, whose failure would be a public calamity,—no mere personal
misfortune. Intellectual distinction, natural eloquence, and the personal charm that made her so marked and attractive a figure, had
brought her into prominence as a leader among progressive women.
If she seemed inclined to take herself a trifle seriously, no one could
wonder, for the demands made upon her were neither few nor slight.
And while a more selfish person might have shown a nice discrimina-
tion in the choice of duties, Ellen, in her gracious readiness to be of
service, accepted as obligations all the greatnesses thrust upon her.
Constantly importuned for utterances, she felt bound to answer all
requests for opinions, till at last, her sense of humour grew weak in
conflict with her strenuousness, she had become an oracle on all matters that were or ought to be of interest to women. And so it happened that when she had been asked to make a speech at the Wom-
en's Convention in Indianapolis, on *The Educational Value of College Life*, she had unhesitatingly consented. But in this instance her
fame and her conscience had brought her face to face with failure, for
on a subject peculiarly suited to her, she could find no words for feelings or ideas.

She was in despair, for not to make the speech would be to play
the traitor to the cause of Woman, and to show the basest ingratitude
to Bryn Mawr, the place that had fitted her for her life work. Taking

herself to task had no effect. She wrote some sentences, read them over, found them vague and inaffective, gushing indeed. She continued to write almost feverishly only to reject sheet after sheet. At length she decided that she had no exact information, neither facts nor figures. That was the trouble. In the discussion of so weighty a matter both were important. Then, almost as an inspiration, it seemed to her, came the thought of Katherine Brewster, also a Bryn Mawrtyr, also interested in woman.

"She is certainly just the person," said Ellen, and she was soon standing on the Brewsters' doorstep. A very systematic maid opened the door and showed Ellen to a small room at the end of the hall. Katherine's quarters had always met with her approval,—the little room in which she waited, communicating as she remembered with a larger room beyond, had about it an air of business and privacy. Though it had for seats only the stiffest of chairs, and for reading matter only the dullest of reports, Ellen's mood led her to envy the uncomfortable and repellent atmosphere. By force of contrast it reminded her of many miserable occasions, when she had tried to feel at ease, while interviewing some ardent reformer in the presence of her humourous if sympathetic family.

She forgot for the time being, what she could not but perceive in her less absorbed moments, that the distinction and notoriety of Katherine was the distinction and notoriety of the Brewster family; and that, in sacrificing the general comfort to the convenience of one, they were exchanging insignificance for importance; while she, however conspicuous personally, was also the daughter of Chief Justice Blake, and was "the image of her mother, the beautiful Polly Meredith." "Not so good-looking though," sighed many an old gentleman, as his thoughts reverted to the triumphs of that beauteous maid in the days when girls broke hearts, rather than conventions.

Wealth and social distinction, good-breeding and beauty were hers without an effort, without a college education; yet she knew well that there was something in her that was due to Bryn Mawr. In striving to express this she had come to Katherine Brewster, sure that from her she would get the explanation.

She had hardly sat down before the door between the rooms opened energetically and the brisk young owner appeared, cheerful and businesslike in manner.

"Oh, Ellen! How do you do? I shall be at leisure," drawing out her watch and considering a moment, "in six or seven minutes."

Without waiting for an answer, Katherine turned back to the other room. She left the door behind her open and Ellen could not but see what was going on. Her disused sense of the ridiculous stirred slightly as she took in the details. Katherine was talking, or rather giving facts, to a young man who was dotting down her words in shorthand. From the scraps of the conversation that reached her, Ellen received a confused impression of myriads of facts marshalled in excellent order. She congratulated herself that she had indeed come to the right person and would find valuable assistance in the clear brain of Katherine Brewster.

At length she caught the words, "I have now given you all the information at my command, and shall trust you to make it interesting to the general public and so prepare the way for our reform." The young man could not linger in face of the finality in her manner, and before he was well out of the door Katherine had turned to her next visitor with brief friendliness.

"I'm glad to see you, Ellen, and can just fit you in between the Committee of Councils and the reporter, who was anxious to get my opinion on the new system for the disposal of garbage. I should like to tell you all about it. It is so absorbing."

"I am afraid I shall have to hold you down to another subject. I need enlightenment as well as the reporter. I have to tell the Women's Congress the value of life in a woman's college. I was sure this subject was one on which I was well informed, till I came to think what I might say,—and lo! commonplaces are all I can utter. I was at a loss what to do,—loath to break my promise, and helpless in my stupidity. Now, can't you give me an idea? I hate to bother you, you are so busy. But it isn't for myself only."

"Well, Ellen, I think I can help you," answered Katherine with the utmost seriousness, "but you will need pencil and paper," rising to get them, "or suppose you sit here," sweeping aside the papers littered over the desk and pointing to the chair in front of it. "I shall have to deal in figures and you might not remember them all."

Then followed a maze of numbers reeled off with surprising readiness, now and then authenticated by a glance at one of the many pigeon-holes. Ellen felt somewhat dazed; but she was conscious that the bewilderment was her contribution for the figures were arranged with precision,—*Health of College Women, Matrimonial Prospects of College Women, The College Woman and the Problem of Domestic Service, The Economic Results of College training for Women*. Valuable facts were quoted from them, facts bristling with suggestions for the capable young woman so utterly mistress of them, but a trifle unmanageable for Ellen till she should have time thoroughly to conquer them.

She was not altogether ungrateful when the servant announced the Committee of Selectmen, and she hastened to show her deference to the fathers of the city by immediate withdrawal.

Katherine's good-bye took the form of advice, "I should certainly deal with the practical value of college life, taking up some line of thought that will show its power to make women effective citizens in the broad sense of the word."

There was no use in going directly home, for she could make nothing of facts so dull, Ellen decided, as she left the house. Besides she had no time to get down to work. It was now four o'clock, and she had promised to be at Edith Warrington's for tea at five. She could go directly there; or, better still, she might find Sara Ford and Augusta Coles at home. Their flat was near by. They would be sure to give her some ideas.

Sara was alone when Ellen reached their rooms, and gave her a warm and ready welcome, of the sort that tempted to friendly chat rather than to weighty discussion. Sara was slight and frail in appearance, and made an immediate appeal to most persons by the wistful expression of her eyes. But for all her seeming delicacy, she was full of nervous strength, and was besides very earnest, almost anxious in her devotion to her duty and in her attitude toward the responsibilities of a college woman.

There was in the room an effect of collision, of an effort to combine the possessions of a gentle, ease-loving nature, with those of one given overmuch to austerity. The room itself, sunny and old-fashioned, went far to reconcile the hostile elements, and the result was inviting, if not harmonious.

Sara had settled Ellen comfortably on the broad window-seat, and was solicitously tucking pillows behind her back, apologizing the while for Augusta's absence. "She has gone to see an authority on labor," Sara explained. "She wanted his opinion on public ownership. She won't be gone long, though."

"How does Augusta excite herself over such questions?" wondered Ellen. Sara smiled absent-mindedly, and then as though pondering, without a shade of remonstrance in her manner, said, "Augusta has the keenest insight into everyday subjects, and the most wonderful grasp of them that I have ever known. I never dare to be amused at Augusta. I can do nothing but admire her. But now, Nell," she continued, drawing her chair nearer the window where Ellen was sitting, "tell me about yourself. You are always doing interesting things. Certainly the world ought to be convinced of the value of college education by the work of such women as you and Augusta."

Ellen's mind was so firmly fixed on the object of her visit that she was unembarrassed by the flattery lavished upon her, and noted only the sympathy in the words. When she had explained her difficulties to Sara, she met with instant comprehension.

"Why, Nellie dear, I know just how you feel," was the prompt response to Ellen's statement. "You are conscious of an overwhelming desire to honour Bryn Mawr, of a responsibility to woman's education, and you would not by a word injure the one or retard the other."

"Of course, I feel that. But what am I going to do? I've thought and thought till I haven't an idea left. Katherine Brewster has loaded me down with statistics, but I need something more. Can't you give me a hint? There is so much of the picturesque in the college life that is not at all frivolous, and yet when I put pen to paper it is gone."

"I am always conscious of just that state of mind," assented Sara, "when I try to express my feeling about college. The beauty of the place, the glamour over everything! One can't describe it."

It was becoming evident to Ellen that Sara was but echoing her own words, was giving sympathy rather than advice. She had just made up her mind to be off, when the door opened to admit Sara's roommate.

A cursory, modern greeting was all that Augusta Barneson Coles vouchsafed her visitor.

"Is there anything I can do for you?" asked Augusta, drawing off her gloves, and with the greatest precision pulling out the fingers. When she had finished this operation she laid the gloves on the table. Augusta maintained, against all comers, that neatness alone was to be considered in dress, and showed herself consistent by appearing at a formal dinner party in an immaculate shirt waist and short skirt. In the obtrusive simplicity of the shapeless coat, the uncompromising hat, the well-hung but skimped skirt, the severely arranged tie, the colour-less hair smoothed in defiance of the wind, the stout shoes and correct stockings, you perceived the care of one who had a character to pre-serve.

Ellen straightened herself and assumed a thrifty exactness in her speech, setting aside preamble and apology; for in talk with Augusta she felt that the amenities of life were worse than wasted, they were insulting.

"Yes, Augusta, tell me what you can say for women's colleges, as distinguished from other modes of training."

"They will redeem the world from its present deplorable condi-tion by teaching women to live by ideas," was the succinct if sweeping assertion.

"I am afraid I don't understand," murmured Ellen.

"By removing them from the sordid pressure of the practical," Augusta went on, "and that at a critical period in the mind's develop-ment and bringing them into an atmosphere of pure ideas, till the concrete no longer exists for them."

This statement seemed somewhat nonsensical to Ellen, but she had come for information and persisted. "That's all very well, but to make it more personal. I can't express what my college education has meant to me. What has it meant to you?"

"Experience meetings of any sort are distasteful to me," answered Augusta brusquely, "they make impossible abstract thought and result in commonplaces of undisciplined sentiment. They bend the idea to the individual, not the individual to the idea."

There was no doubt that Augusta had given all that was in her power and that Ellen would only lose time by urging her to closer def-inition. So far she had received opinions almost irreconcilable one with the other, the practical views of Katherine and the abstractions of Augusta. She was indeed amused rather than disappointed at the fail-ure of her visit. How absurd she had been to expect fertile suggestions from Sara, always ready to reflect the mood of her companion—a qual-ity often soothing and endearing but hardly useful in moments of per-plexity;—or from Augusta with her futile theories and ridiculous jar-gon.

She had still one hope, Bertha Christie, who had gathered about her a group of Bryn Mawr graduates, all anxious to indulge the scho-lastic passion. Research and literature occupied them for the most part; but, in the intervals of study, they cultivated self-consciousness and held dress-rehearsals that they might perfect themselves in the parts selected. Phrase-making was their pastime and tricks of face and manner their delight. Their duty to themselves led them to withdraw from their families, thus liberating themselves from the exigencies of an unappreciative society. So sedulous were these artists in life to free themselves from tyranny to the individual that they regarded all out-side demands as impertinent intrusions. They courted criticism and experience and craved æsthetic satisfaction.

The only one of the band at home when Ellen was shown in, was Bertha Christie. Had she been seen in the midst of commonplace surroundings, dressed in a less studied fashion, she would in all likeli-hood have passed unnoticed. But the clinging folds of her dress, ex-quisite in colour and texture, the deliberately loosened hair, the poise of the head, and the languid grace of motion as she moved forward to greet Ellen, suggested something of the romantic, something of the ascetic, with just a seasoning of coquetry. She had the artistic temper-ament, but abilities critical rather than creative. She read poetry but measured life by her intellect. Hers was a disposition susceptible to impressions, but cruel in the analysis of them.

Her expression of indifference became one of scornful amuse-ment as she listened to Ellen's earnest setting forth of her errand. A skilled fencer in words she succeeded in parrying the insistent queries, without revealing the triviality of her ideas. The impression left on El-len's mind by this conversation was really disturbing. Up to this point she had no doubts about the value of college life, but now she won-dered if there were not more to be said against it than for it. Was it not responsible for the selfishness and affectation of Bertha Christie? She looked at the clock on a near-by steeple and saw that she was al-ready late for her engagement with Edith. In her annoyance at her wasted effort she was not sorry to think that at her next stopping-place she might dismiss business from her thoughts and enjoy the consola-tion and diversion she was sure to find.

It was significant of her attitude that, although she had meant all along to drop in on Edith, on her way home, and knew besides that she was certain to find one or two more of her college friends, she had no thought of them in connection with her speech. She had uncon-sciously drifted into imagining, as did all outsiders, that Augusta Coles and Bertha Christie were the types and her own friends the anomalies among college women. Her friendships and her activities were no longer brought into contact. So long as Ellen was looking for companionship, she still showed herself capable of appreciating wisdom as well as cleverness, good sense as well as originality; but just so soon as she desired enlightenment, she forgot that her own friends might hold opinions worthy of consideration, and singled out the eccentric or visionary among her acquaintances. In doing so she was not consciously seeking singularity, she was rather showing her instinctive reverence for experience. Having become something of a doctrinaire, she went for her instruction to those more advanced than herself.

Had Edith Warrington been true to what seemed to Ellen the best in her, she might have been set among the sages, but Edith had voluntarily forfeited all right to be considered really earnest, for after she had determined to devote her life to study, she had been turned aside by a mere trifle. In the second year of her post-graduate study, she had had a call from an old lady whom she had always found most entertaining and had been bored with the random gossip so delightful hitherto.

"It's the last straw," she said, in talking to one of her friends of the occurrence, "when Mrs. Astruther bores me there's something the matter. I've noticed an indifference to everything but my work growing upon me of late, but have ignored it. This shock has brought me to my senses and shows me that I prefer people to things." She was urged not to generalize too hastily, by the friends who were eager to see her fulfil her promise as a scholar. She had now been married about five years, and, because the memory of her scholarship was still fresh, she was spoken of as one lost past recovery; for, though she never lost her student ways, she was no longer called a student.

When Ellen came within sight of the house, she heard some one tap on the pane and on looking up saw Edith signalling to her not to ring.

"Here you are at last, Nell," was her greeting. "I was looking for you. What kept you so late? Some old committee?"

"Oh, I'm dead tired. I have had a miserable afternoon."

"You poor thing! Come along and be amused. Louise and Evelyn are here. They're having a heated discussion about matrimony. It's a bit personal and very funny."

"Louise and Evelyn? It must be absurd."

"Yes, they think they're talking on broad general principles, but they're just talking about Dick Fisher and Mr. Brandon."

"You know him?" asked Ellen. "I've never met him and since Evelyn's engagement was announced I've been curious about him."

"Oh, he is a very nice fellow—really charming."

"But not good enough for Evelyn, I'm sure."

"They never are, are they, Nell?" and Edith turned with an amused smile.

"No, not even Mr. Warrington," laughed Ellen. "I don't agree about him yet."

When they reached the little study, Ellen nodded to the two girls sitting near the window and flung herself into an easy chair by the tea table, glad to rest her mind with a counter distraction. She knew the disputants well and felt as much at home with them as with Edith.

Louise Fisher had been her room-mate at college, distinguished for her common sense and independent ways and a warm advocate of the business career for women, all women married or single. Many a satirical picture had Ellen drawn in those days, of Louise's ideal of domestic happiness. But Louise had become engaged before she graduated, to a man immeasurably her superior in mental ability, and she had settled down to echoing his opinions. Ellen often wondered if no ghosts sat opposite to Louise at the breakfast table; but she could not disturb her by any amount of banter.

Evelyn Ames, the other disputant, had been an enigma at college. She had attracted many on first acquaintance; but had baffled them at the point where acquaintance ripens into intimacy. No one dared call herself Evelyn's friend, except such as were content with the formal graciousness of her ways. And yet she had been a force in college life, had shown both courage and enthusiasm at critical moments.

She had recently announced her engagement, and was naïve in her disclosures of her own feelings in the present discussion. She was thoroughly at her ease with her companions; for since she had left college, she had surprised many, whom she had before held at a distance, into very real friendships, taking them unawares by her affection for Bryn Mawr and its associations. These three had discovered that her inaptitude for fellowship at college was the result of a former starvation of her affections. The daughter of a widow, a woman of small means, of cold nature and social ambition, Evelyn had not been allowed to find out the softer side of her nature, till she had been sent to Bryn Mawr by a rich and domineering relative.

When Edith and Ellen joined them, Louise was saying, "The only way is to try to divert his mind from his work."

"But that doesn't seem to me at all the nicest way," said Evelyn. "I think you ought to be able to help a man in his work."

"At that rate," said Edith, as she poured out a cup of tea, "Ellen should marry a public man and help him write his——"

"Yes," sniffed Louise contemptuously, "like Mrs. Jones, Dick says——"

"Oh, Nell," and Evelyn turned quickly to Ellen, "somebody told me about the speech you're to make. What a splendid chance you've got."

"I don't know about that," answered Ellen, "it's the hardest thing I ever had to do. I can't for the life of me——"

"But just think," interrupted Evelyn, "it means Bryn Mawr. That's what we think of when we think of college. Oh! I wish I could just for once say what I think of the dear place. But I never can talk about it in a sensible way."

"Just as well," put in Edith, "it's one of the things it doesn't pay to be sensible about."

"Edith, what do you mean?" interjected Louise, "when you speak in public you can't talk twaddle. Dick says, common sense is the only thing that holds people."

"He's faithful to his opinions anyway," answered Edith with a friendly nod, "you've just as much as ever."

"But, Nell," asked Evelyn, leaning forward in her interest, "what are you going to say?"

"That's what I don't know. I've gone from pillar to post trying to find out and——"

"No wonder you're weary," said Edith, "wasting your time that way. Why on earth didn't you ask us? Please tell us where you did go."

"Oh, to several places," answered Ellen evasively. "I never thought of bothering you people, you have so many outside things to attend to."

"Yes to be sure, husbands and children and all the——"

"You know that isn't what I mean," objected Ellen, setting down her teacup. "You always say you aren't interested in movements."

"Oh, no!" corrected Edith, "not movements."—

"Well, anyway I didn't succeed with the other people. 'College training fits us to be citizens'; 'college teaches us to live by ideas'; 'college is of value to none but those gifted with a susceptibility for the exquisite refinements of the intellectual existence.' What am I to do with that?"

Edith and Evelyn exchanged amused glances, while Louise looked scornful. Ellen continued, "I have to think how my words will affect Bryn Mawr, and also how they will strike my audience."

"Don't forget yourself," said Edith. "You've a way of leaving a bit of yourself behind when you get to work."

"Oh, it will come to you, don't fear," broke in Evelyn. "You do all that sort of thing so well, you'll be sure to make a hit. You couldn't help it talking about Bryn Mawr. If only I could do it. My four years there made life worth living."

"Come now, Evelyn," said Edith teasingly, "it will never do for you to say things like that, and you just engaged. Please think of poor Mr. Brandon. He'll get to hate Bryn Mawr, and I won't blame him a scrap. You must——"

"That has nothing to do with it," protested Evelyn, looking embarrassed, "but I know nothing could have been at all as it is if I hadn't gone there. With me the trouble wasn't so much a dearth of resources as a lack of opportunity for devotion. When I got to college I found that the thing demanded of me was devotion to Bryn Mawr. Every one expected it and I gave myself up to serving the first thing that needed me."

"But that wasn't anything in Bryn Mawr," objected Louise, "that was you."

"Don't you think," interposed Edith, "that the personal romance of our lives takes the place of all impersonal romance of that sort in time?"

"Perhaps," assented Evelyn slowly, "but it is the one romance that hasn't to rub up against realities. We lived there in a world of our own creation—a land of dreams. Our dreams for Bryn Mawr may always be realized; they are never shown to be impossible."

"Well, really," exclaimed Louise, "you seem to be getting very high falutin, all of you. My feeling about college is that if it hadn't been for my friends it would have been a hateful place—all hard work and nothing else. It's the friendships you make there that count."

"To be sure they count," said Edith, "but you might say the same of boarding-school. I know what it is. It's the student government."

"Now just listen to that," cried Ellen, "you're as bad as other people, you don't agree at all. You, Edith, talk of self-government, but that isn't general. And I can't tie myself down to Bryn Mawr. We all think Bryn Mawr the best of——"

"Twenty years hence this weather
May tempt us from office stools;
We may be slow on the feather,
And seem to the boys old fools.
But we'll still swing together
And swear by the best of schools,"[4]

sang a merry voice in the doorway and with one accord the girls sprang to their feet to welcome the singer. But she continued serenely,—"The same idea may be found in the lines of another well-known song:

"'When the cares of life o'ertake us—'"[5]

The last lines were lost in the vehemence with which Ellen and Edith greeted the newcomer.

"You piece of absurdity," urged Edith impatiently, "stop your mimicry and tell us how you got here."

"Without adventure, my excitable Edith, till I came upon this strange gathering, perhaps the strangest gathering ever known to the scientist,—for as Leuwenhoek[6] says——" The change of voice in the last

---

[4] These are William Johnson Cory's words for the eighth stanza of the Eton Boating Song of Eton College (despite the name, a boarding school for upper-class high school-aged boys) in England, first performed in 1863.

[5] The first line of the Alma Mater song of many a school; the last line often plays on the school colors. As applied to Bryn Mawr, the full hypothetical lyrics might go:

When the cares of life o'ertake us,
mingling fast our locks with gray.
Should our clearest hopes betray us,
false fortunes fall away.
Still we banish care and sadness,
in the darkest of the night,
And recall our days of gladness
'neath the Yellow and the White.

[6] Antonie van Leeuwenhoek (1632-1723), considered the first microbiologist.

words, and the immediate response from her listeners showed a traditional joke. But she went on immediately, "I'm on my way to Bryn Mawr and I dropped in to remind you that you've all promised to bear me company. I was afraid you might forget. A trip there from Philadelphia is less of an undertaking than one from Emmonsville, Montana. And I'm going to pass the night with you, fair Ellen. I wrote to you warning you of my intention about two weeks ago. My trunk is already at your house, and I have been there; but was sent to bring you home. Your mother was afraid you would forget you were to dine with Mrs. Boughton and help her with a Dean or a Bishop,—something architectural and impressive."

"I had forgotten all about it and I haven't a minute to lose," said Ellen, as she and Marjorie hurried off amid the protests of the others.

Ellen begged Marjorie to come upstairs with her and amuse her while she dressed; but Marjorie refused to talk, insisting on hearing all about Ellen's visits of the afternoon. She passed her comment on the characters in the narrative, comment genial, friendly, sympathetic, till Ellen came to Bertha Christie's part. On a sudden Marjorie's indignation blazed out.

"Ellen, is it that you have failed to understand Bryn Mawr, or that you have willfully misunderstood? You have accepted the judgment of the outside world and have treated those freaks as representatives of Bryn Mawr. Have you forgotten how they were ignored, jeered at, anything but accepted by everybody but a few freshmen? They defied college spirit, mocked at common sense and still do. And the world sets them down as types! Bertha Christie with her menagerie of intimates intolerant of the commonplace! I could pity them if people like you didn't make them of so much importance."

"Intolerant, maybe I am," in answer to a feeble protest from Ellen, "I'm rather proud of being intolerant of a set of sophisticated hermit-crabs, a few puling nuns who've gone to school to the melancholy Jacques. No wonder I hear queer things about Bryn Mawr when you go to them for ideas and pass by Edith and Evelyn and a host of others. It's enough to make one turn cynic. Tolerance! Tolerance of evil, breadth of mind it calls itself, is the most discouraging thing I meet with. And yet how absurd it all is. You, so well-balanced, so lofty in your aims, going to those geese to learn wisdom——"

"They're not geese," protested Ellen at length, "they're unusually clever girls."

"'A goose,' please remember," quoted Marjorie, regaining her temper with the reassertion of her sense of humour, "is none the less a goose, though sun and stars be minced to yield him stuffing! You'd better be off or you'll have to apologize to the Bishop for keeping him from his dinner."

II

Greatly to her astonishment Ellen found that she had fallen to the Bishop's care at dinner. She was not, however, easily appalled by distinguished people, and she chatted lightly to the stranger. His beautiful face, benignant and merry, set her completely at her ease,—the secure ease of the American woman, it seemed to him as he made mental notes of the effect produced by the exquisite dress, the vivacity and readiness, the almost boyish frankness, the worldly wisdom. And all the time he wondered why there recurred to him the thought of a serious nature, an intellectual nature, free from worldliness and triviality.

Ellen was giving herself up to the enjoyment of the moment, giving her best to a listener so responsive and stimulating and she was all the more ready to do so because of the concentrated thought of the day. But she was not to escape for long, for she heard her companion say, "You have been a student at Bryn Mawr, they tell me, Miss Blake, and I have been greatly interested in hearing so; for I think it a most lovely spot, quite an ideal sort of place. Its airs of age are very clever too, very deceptive. It impressed me as an old place. An almost reverential feeling stirred me, so marked was the sense of dignity. It is in a word academic. Everywhere one may see that bewildering mixture of history and aspiration."

"We can't help feeling a little proud that after so few years of existence it should begin to be impressive as well as beautiful," said Ellen, who hardly welcomed the return to the subject that had engrossed her thoughts so long, though she could not resist the enthusiasm of one familiar with the English universities.

"Of course, in this country one never wonders at rapidity of growth, but I must confess that æsthetic charm does not always accompany it. That delightful president of yours has secured both."

"She is a worker of wonders. She has plans for the place now that exceed all our dreams."

"Of course years may mellow the ugliest spot and association endear it, but after all 'virtue is loveliest in lovely guise.' The gift of beauty is not to be despised. Even the most casual visitor must acknowledge a spell in that college of yours altogether independent of the mysterious charm that you who know it intimately find for yourselves,—to some degree what I am sure people would find in my own university were they to go there ignorant of its wealth of history. But they are outsiders," he continued musingly, almost as though he had forgotten the existence of the girl to whom he was talking, "they see only the outward show, they are forever shut out from a share in that spirit that is the immortal part of the university, that persists in spite of change."

The old man's memories awoke at these words, and in his reminiscences he unfolded for Ellen picture after picture of that old world school, and flattered her with a sight of the thing her Alma Mater might become. For she listened to tales that made distant things seem real and present to her, stories of the frailties of men whose names had been beacons to her intellect. Her emotions were stirred by the tender humour that summoned up for her the personalities that had touched his own boyhood, and had left their impress on the life of Oxford.

The bishop's attention was challenged by a gentleman across the table with a question on South Africa, and for the rest of the evening Ellen shared her friend with the other guests.

Before she left she found a chance to tell Mrs. Boughton how delightful her companion had been. "Well, Ellen, to be candid," with an indulgent smile at the girl whom she liked in spite of her brains, "I should not have honoured you so much had he not asked to have you for a neighbour. But you needn't lay the credit to your attractions. I was running over the people he would meet this evening and when I came to you, that he might not expect an angel, I mentioned your only faults,—that you had been to college and spelled woman with a large W. But I told him that as a rule you kept these peculiarities in the background. However it was your having been to college that interested him, for he wanted to see what sort of women Bryn Mawr turned out. Of course I told him he couldn't judge by you—you were an exception—that he would have to see a few specimens like your friend Miss Christie or Augusta Barneson Coles."

As she drove home Ellen's thoughts turned to Marjorie Heywood and her plans for the next day. The talk at dinner had decided Ellen to go with the others. Though she lived so near, she found little pleasure in going out to Bryn Mawr nowadays, for everything seemed changed and she felt nothing but resentment that the past should have been so easily forgotten, its ways so quickly superseded.

Her careless reading of Marjorie's letter had made her arrival a surprise, and Ellen experienced a sense of relief at Marjorie's appearance. Her relief showed how apprehensive she had been of the changes possible in ten years' time, and above all in a ten years so trying as those that Marjorie had passed through. Just when she had seemed well started in her chosen work she had had to give up everything and care for a worthless brother. She had had to fight poverty for herself and him, and for him disease and evil. The cheerful letters that had come to Ellen now and then, had brought her little satisfaction, they were so impersonal. It had been in vain that Edith reminded her that Marjorie had always been impersonal, reticent. Putting herself into everything she did and said was her way of talking about herself. It had been in vain too that Edith contended that Marjorie's enthusiasm for righteousness and humorous freshness of mind were her safeguard against old age. "Marjorie will be just the same," she maintained, "when she is a hundred years old." To-night for the first time, Ellen believed her. Ten years! Could it be ten years? And Marjorie still the same, the old spirit of raillery gleaming in her eyes, the irresistible quiver at the corners of the mouth?

Ellen found her mother and Marjorie in the full swing of a good talk. They had been linked in their sympathetic understanding of one another since early in freshman year, when Marjorie had spent a Sunday with Ellen. And to-night they had no remembrance of the interval that had passed since they had last been together. Ellen longed to throw herself into one of the easy chairs and share in the ardour of conversation; but she remembered her speech.

"If I am to fall in with your plan, and I am afraid I am too weak to defy your indomitable will, I must write that wretched speech to-night. I don't dare trust myself to write it at Bryn Mawr with you to beguile me," was her answer to Marjorie's entreaties that she should stop and tell them all about her evening.

"Oh, sit up all night, if you'll get to Bryn Mawr by doing it," answered Marjorie with a nod to Mrs. Blake who was about to remonstrate. "I'll assist you by the subtle influence of my presence and read the while.

"What do I want to read? Oh, anything at all, thank you, Mrs. Blake,—something that will keep me from interrupting Ellen. Yes, that's just the thing," and she took the book that Mrs. Blake handed her and started upstairs.

As the girls reached the room Ellen said, "I've a good mind to give the whole thing up. I'm perfectly hopeless about it."

"You'll do nothing of the kind," asserted Marjorie. "You'll just sit down there and write."

"It will be a perfunctory business at that rate," objected Ellen, "I don't feel as though I could write a word."

"Never mind that," retorted Marjorie, "but just see that you get through with it to-night. A body can't get any good of you with it on your mind. And that's one of the things I came on for."

With that Marjorie opened her book and Ellen sat down to her task. It went slowly at first. She wrote little and that with constant reference to her notes. But after a time she seemed to find the thoughts coming more quickly.

Marjorie's book did not seem to hold her attention. Her thoughts seemed borne beyond it, and her eyes wandered about the room, noting the restfulness of the golden brown on the walls, the preponderance of etchings—landscapes for the most part—the low bookcase stretching the full length of the wall, the ornaments, obviously the choice of one more susceptible to form than to colour. There was in the room nothing brilliant, nothing conspicuous. Taking in the details, her glance came at length to rest on Ellen herself as she bent over the old-fashioned desk. She was turned so that Marjorie could see a little more than her profile. And Marjorie's expression was one of affectionate amusement as she watched the serious, almost stern lines of the face, the gravity in the eyes, when they were occasionally raised.

For some time Marjorie observed her closely and then broke in upon the silence with,—"I'm drifting irresistibly to conversation or drowsiness, I don't know which, but in any case I'd much better away to bed. So good-night and good luck."

Then just as she reached the door she turned laughingly to Ellen and said, "Your hair is just as nice as ever; but I'm afraid you've got the world tied to your little finger."

But Ellen merely nodded and smiled at the sound of Marjorie's voice, not hearing one word of the taunt.

III

Marjorie had had her way and the five friends were now spending the last day of their visit to Bryn Mawr, as they had spent the others, picking up old threads and discovering new ones.

The changes since their day were many and to Marjorie, seeing them for the first time, they seemed like personal affronts, rousing in her that passion of resentment which is the lunacy of the graduate. The old gate was done away with. The old road no longer existed. A long stretch of buildings struck her eye unfamiliarly. Taylor had shrunk itself among the trees and its dear ugliness was retired from the gaze of approaching visitors. But the alterations were so skillful that the alumnæ soon felt an admiring ownership in them and quickly embraced the changes.

Almost the only familiar figures to be seen were those of college servants there since the beginning, one of whom, William, once well-nigh universal in his activities, was now so highly differentiated that he seemed to do nothing but carry the mails. He was a repository of traditions, and he delighted forlorn alumnæ by his air of proprietorship in the past as well as in the present. Small wonder that, when they found their doings sunk into a mere tradition and marked the shortness of memory and self-importance of the undergraduates, they turned for cheer to William's flattery and refused to consider its ambiguities.

"No, no, miss, none of our young ladies now are like the young ladies when you were here. In your time they certainly was young ladies.

"And your name, miss? It's the same I suppose, I'm afraid to call any of you by name, there's so many married, you see, and they might be offended if I didn't remember the gentleman's name, you see. I keep track of you all by reading the list of names and who's dead and married. Talking of marriages, miss, so Dr. ___ is married. Well, he's the last of our professors I'd a thought of marrying. Well, changes is changes, miss, when all's said and done."

On this their last afternoon, Susan Everett and Beatrice O'Hara had joined the five where they were sitting under the cherry tree in front of Taylor. Their talk was of the undergraduates and the zest with which they listened to tales of those first days.

"Their seeming disregard of us and our doings is the result of ignorance, not of indifference," Edith was saying, "but their curiosity is now thoroughly aroused."

"Oh, yes indeed," groaned Marjorie, "they've decided they'll collect the traditions and if you've the age of Methuselah and the memory of Macaulay, they wind you up and you can be doing nothing at all but telling them stories. And you've to stop and explain to them who the Polyglot is and the Gifted, and even I can't quite make clear to them those treasures of individuality. All you get for your pains is, 'Oh yes! one of the professors.'"

Her plaint seemed to be justified, for across from Pembroke some girls came running and when they saw the group under the tree, one of them called out,—"Oh, here you are, Miss Heywood! May we not come and learn some more history?"

And as though Marjorie's consent were a foregone conclusion, they sat down on the grass at her feet and settled themselves as children will for the treat in store.

"Come, Tommie, tell us a story and play the fool for us, as you used to do," said Susan Everett lapsing into the old name and desirous that Marjorie should assume her old character.

"I should have drifted naturally into my accustomed rôle, had you kept still a moment; but introductory remarks are death to spontaneity. And, like Amanda Jones, I want my little fun spontaneous.

"Now, you never knew Amanda Jones," she continued to the undergraduates, "but by that historic utterance she deprived you of a custom. Did you ever think why you never had a class-day at Bryn Mawr? You know you never have had one, and if you ever do the ghost of Amanda Jones will haunt the campus.

"It was the year we graduated, and we," indicating her companions, "had been sitting up into the small hours arranging for a class-day. The first class had gone out in solemn dignity, but we craved something more; we would have a class-day. We had an elaborate program made out, amusing, but academic, without doubt the cleverest entertainment that has ever been or ever will be. We had written an inimitable parody of the *Clouds*,—so funny, so much funnier than anything Aristophanes ever did. Humour so subtle was never heard. We couldn't read it ourselves without weeping with laughter. Well, the parts were assigned, the costumes half made, the invitations sent out, when of a sudden a class meeting was called at Amanda's request. As soon as preliminaries were over she arose, made a telling arraignment of class-day, referred touchingly to former graduations at Bryn Mawr, and then she, who had never even gone to an entertainment, much less invented one, paused dramatically, and slowly enunciated, 'we've always had our little fun spontaneous!' She carried the day, and still carries it, and there is no such thing as class-day at Bryn Mawr."

"Amanda wasn't about when we were practicing for our comb-orchestra," laughed Beatrice. "Poor Amanda! She didn't know that the deliberations beforehand were half the fun."

"Do you remember," asked Ellen, "the evening we spent sitting in the trunk-room in Merion, helping Alice Marston write the *Professor?*"

"Dear me, I had forgotten," sighed Louise, "and I don't think anything has ever seemed really funny since that."

"The sad part of it is," continued Evelyn, "that the warning in the motto we used would now be a necessity. Who but ourselves would understand those jokes? What was the motto?" to an inquiring freshman,

"Quae jocum suspiciet, eam oportet ridere;
Quae non, oportet aliis ridentibus ridere.
Ne lacrima!
Quot intellixistis?"[7]

"Don't apologize for talking Latin, Evelyn," said Marjorie, with a comical glance at the group, "it's like our mother tongue."

"That was the way the Latin lecture used to begin," explained Ellen, for the benefit of the undergraduates. "You see we used to have lectures in Latin as a sort of elective."

"That sounds impressive; it did to me when I first heard it," responded Marjorie, "but those Latin lectures were the most humorous things you could imagine. You watched the Polyglot's face, and you knew when to laugh and when to weep, and you were a little dull if you didn't understand enough to raise your hand when he called out 'Quot intellixistis?'

---

[7]   Latin for "She who suspects a joke must laugh; others must laugh uproariously at she who does not. No crying! How many of you got it?"

"Do you remember the one on Irish bulls? In your honour wasn't it, Pat?" turning to Beatrice O'Hara, whose vaunted Irish blood was evident in her speech.

"I wish I'd kept a record of Pat's bulls," remarked Susan. "I often feel as though one of them was just the tonic I needed."

"Never mind," answered Beatrice, good-humouredly, "I once saw through one all by myself. That time I told you I was carrying a stool with me because I had to stand up."

"I often think of the way the Gifted chuckled, because you would say 'whenever a man died,'" added Ellen.

"I didn't deserve his ridicule; for I was the only person capable of understanding what he meant by his favourite 'on a mutual hand,' or of appreciating the beautiful idea of his 'tell all that you don't know about this subject.'"

"Oh, Marjorie," exclaimed Edith, "have you forgotten how you disgraced yourself just because you thought you noticed the joke introducing expression on a learned lecturer's face? You would go to the German lecture on Ulfilas, thinking it wise to make the most of all opportunities for getting up your German for your orals."

"Not a bit of it," interrupted Marjorie, "I came to myself to find the distinguished guests and the members of the Faculty gazing at me as though I were crazy, and you pinching me black and blue. And all because I had worked myself into hysterics of laughter over the Lord's Prayer in Gothic."[8]

---

[8] The text of the Lord's Prayer, in transliterated 4th century Gothic (an extinct Germanic language spoken, of course, by the original Goths), runs as follows:

Atta unsar thu in himinam,	*Our Father who art in heaven,*
weihnai namo thein.	*hallowed be thy name.*
qimai thiudinassus theins.	*Thy kingdom come.*
wairthai wilja theins,	*Thy will be done,*
swe in himina jah ana airthai.	*on earth as it is in heaven.*
hlaif unsarana thana sinteinan	*Give us this day*
gif uns himma daga.	*our daily bread.*
jah aflet uns thatei skulans sijaima,	*Forgive us our trespasses,*
swaswe jah weis afletun	*as we forgive those*
thaim skulam unsaraim.	*who trespass against us.*
jah ni briggais uns in fraistubnjai,	*Lead us not into temptation,*
ak lausei uns af thamma ubilin;	*but deliver us from evil;*
unte theine ist thiudangardi	*for thine is the kingdom*
jah mahts jah wulthus in aiwins.	*the power and the glory forever.*
amen.	*Amen.* (cont'd)

"Wasn't it queer in those days when everything was new?" inquired one of the audience.

"My dear child there never was a time when everything was new, and I know what I'm talking about, for I was the first freshman that ever spent a night in Bryn Mawr, and I then learned that Bryn Mawr already had a history that was venerable, customs that were inviolable. That first night I learned the Manus Bryn Mawrensium[9] and the Maid of Bryn Mawr. I was early taught the tradition of the sacredness of the Harriton family cemetery, taken there by two sponsors, who felt the necessity of impressing us, the newcomers, with the past.

"In that stretch of woodland," here her voice took on a sentimental tone, "known as the Vaux woods, and still frequented by Bryn Mawr students, there lies nestling among the trees a secluded burying ground. Grey walls of ancient date bound it within narrow compass. The masonry sturdily defiant of time, has been mellowed by a growth of moss and lichen. To any eye a picturesque spot! In its calm but cheerful solitude, no inhospitable resting-place! You feel in a sense possessors of that place; you are aware that in some subtle manner it belongs to you; but fully to comprehend your own feelings you must hear the droll, though sentimental reminiscence of the first class of Bryn Mawr; you must picture to yourselves a group of students on the worn steps and the nervous, enthusiastic figure of that 'learned doctor,' as he walks up and down in front of them, declaiming ore rotundo[10] and with all possible expression, the parting of Hector and Andromache.[11] Yes, he taught us Horace," answering a question from one of the groups on the grass. "Oh, you have no such classes now. I couldn't imagine college without his Horace class."

"How we had to work in it, though," sighed Louise.

"Oh yes, but you know we always had his permission to shirk all other work that we might do his," came from Beatrice.

"And at last we had to protest," continued Edith. "Had we done all that was expected of us, we should never have gone to bed. Our protests passed seemingly unheeded, till one day just before Thanks-

---

I must leave it to the reader's judgment to determine to what extent this might justify "hysterics of laughter"—if, indeed, any such justification is needed.

[9] The 1889 class song, written in Latin by Professor Paul Shorey.

[10] Latin, literally "with a round mouth"; that is, eloquently.

[11] An episode in Homer's *Iliad*.

giving, the Polyglot entered the room, one shoulder heaved on high with the great pile of books he held under his arm. Having as usual begun his lecture in the corridor, he was saying as he came inside the door, 'I have with me a most interesting find, a manuscript Latin poem, unexpectedly come into my possession. I shall write it on the board and then ask some one to volunteer with a translation.' Then standing on tiptoe, at times jumping so that he might write at the very top of the blackboard, he began to copy some verses, but long before he had finished, the class was convulsed with laughter. For it was a graceful little apology for overworking us."

"When I think of Bryn Mawr," said Marjorie, "few things have left so vivid an impression on my mind as his class-room. I was under the spell of literature from the moment I heard him give out his first parallel passage. There was in his classes a magical exhilaration never to be forgotten. And to think you poor things don't know anything about it!

"It must seem very different to you now," put in a senior, sympathetically.

"To be sure it does, and I think nothing strikes me more than the light-hearted way in which you do things that we didn't dare to do for fear of bringing down rules on our heads. Like our ancestors we were constantly 'snuffing tyranny.'"

"Hadn't you self-government then?" asked a freshman in amazement.

"We had no government of any sort, and no despotism could have been more compelling than the nameless fear that hung over us, that we might some day do something that would lead some one to take away our liberty."

"I have always regretted the establishment of self-government," said Elizabeth Gordon, a graduate who was to receive her Ph. D. the next day.

"Not at all, not at all," Marjorie hastened to declare. "You were always so immersed in work that you never bothered with other people; but those of us that thought it our duty to keep an eye on the freshmen found our hands full. Why the trips that I have made with my Memorabilia under my arm to administer sugar-coated pellets of college-spirit have cost me many a good mark."

The reminiscences had filled the afternoon, and now the college-bell rang out, warning the various groups that dinner-time was at hand.

With an apologetic laugh Marjorie started up, saying as she walked along, "Six o'clock, and I've talked almost all afternoon! Well! Well! 'Tis but a sign of age."

"Age, you goose," laughed Edith, "weren't you always the 'garrulous particle'?"

"Well, weakness then, and a mistaken notion that there is no place like Bryn Mawr."

IV

The beauty of the long June evening was not to be resisted, and as soon as dinner was over, the students hurried out of doors. An air of relaxation was everywhere noticeable. Those fagged out by examinations gained cheer and liveliness from the more careless, or loitered about in unregarded lassitude not disturbed by any sense of obligation as contributors to the brimming talk of their companions. It was the perfection of easy intercourse where every sentence is a free-will offering.

However far the little knots of good company might wander, they sooner or later gathered about the steps of Taylor Hall to listen to the senior singing. The effect was almost like a stage setting in its perfection, the grey buildings, the intense green of the grass, the blossoms on the trees, the dresses of the girls, the group upon the steps, with the rays of the setting sun falling full upon it. This custom of singing on the steps was an innovation on the manners of the first years, but an innovation picturesque and pathetic. Its pathos touched the group of alumnæ standing at a little distance from the steps. Throughout the afternoon they had almost fancied themselves students again; now they had stepped aside and had become mere spectators, while the seniors were making the most of their last days.

Before the singing stopped darkness had crept upon the scene. Taking advantage of it Ellen slipped away unnoticed and wandered down the hillside. As she heard the strange voices singing the old songs, she suddenly perceived how far she had drifted away from her college days—from all that had been revived by the chatter of the afternoon. She could not but feel that Marjorie's power of awakening those trifling memories, and Edith's quick response to her whims and sallies, her humorous allusions indicated not a less, but a greater share in all that was vital and permanent than any she could claim for all her seriousness. A passionate regret rushed over her, aware now that in her hurry, her business, her very faithfulness, she had lost, almost past recovery, many of the privileges that had been hers; that, in her pursuit of ends, worthy enough to be sure, she had made no demands on the really precious things in her experience at college. For in this moment of reflection, those trivial and petty reminiscences, mere accidents in their student-life, became for her the summons to an act of recollection.

She had strolled across the daisy field and was standing on the brow of the hill looking out toward the west. The moon had risen. Seen in its light the sweep of landscape seemed to her more picturesque, fuller of appeal to the imagination. Details were lost sight of, contrasts of light and shade emphasized. The slope before her lay in the full moonlight. Beyond it a clump of trees showed dark against the lucent sky. In the farther distance the hills were wrapped in a soft mist, brightened here and there by the gleams from the clustered houses. The familiar scene was full of remembrances, but remembrances for the most part of her friendship for Marjorie and Edith. Long tramps across those hills had been their favourite exercise through the winter. The daisy field, the haunt of idle moments in the warm days of spring or autumn, had also been for them a special sort of study, reserved for choicest reading. Toward it too they had always wandered after the Sunday evening meeting. As they walked along their talk would drift from the subject of the evening to things more personal, closer to their hearts, their individual perplexities, their individual faiths. Each one was then at her best, in the light of sympathy, showing herself as good or as noble as she really was. Those conversations, assumed to her kindled imagination, an actuality, a power, hitherto unperceived, becoming not only the record of their preferences in all matters great or small, their criticism of the activities and the thoughts of their own little world, but also the measure of their share in it. The little world thus recalled to her, had, she was beginning to remember, its care for holiness, for truth, for courage, and it had too its care for orderliness and beauty in its very frivolities—and there had been a discipline really stimulating even in that. The genius of the place expressing itself in this care showed itself in light-hearted frolic no less than in scholastic endeavor, for it determined the way in which things were done rather than actual achievements, thus uniting in voluntary submission to its influence those whom individual powers separated from one another, informing them with its spirit, till it became a part of them, not to be changed without the loss of something individual.

How vivid it all was, how persistent, yet how baffling its secret! Why could she not penetrate this secret and possess it? But as before she could neither arrest nor depict the ideas that were passing to and fro in her mind. Her thoughts flew to her speech. In it she had ignored everything but the definite, the tangible, and in so doing she had failed. Yet, even if she could seize the sentiment and translate it into words, she dreaded misapprehension—she could not forget her audience.

"Oh, here you are, Ellen," Marjorie broke in on her reverie, "I've just been singing your praises. It seems there are difficulties in the way of self-government, and I thought I'd help them by giving them a bit of our experience. So I told how you brought us through that bitter time, when we so nearly lost our liberties. As I told them I realized as never before how impossible it is to pass on experience. I could see before me the faces of the girls so drawn, so stern, with that pitiful sternness that only young faces catch; and then I seemed to hear Dr. Rhoads[12] in chapel that next morning, reading to us that chapter about Grace and Law; and I could remember just how he stopped and looked at us after he read the words,—'*For sin shall not have dominion over you; for ye are not under the law but under grace. What then? Shall we sin because we are not under the law, but under grace? God forbid,*'[13]—and then went on to tell us that he believed that those words expressed our spirit and that as long as that spirit guided us we could be trusted to govern ourselves. It seems strange that while the impression of that time will never fade from our minds, we can pass on nothing but the tradition. There is no Dr. Rhoads now," she continued after a pause, "and I think I miss him more than I do any one else. He always used to gather up the events of our life here and put them into their proper relations."

"Yes, he entered with all his heart into the college spirit just as though he were one of us," agreed Edith.

"And for that very reason," said Ellen, "no part of his influence is lost. That spirit is the touchstone for all of us. However variable it is the one thing that persists and, so far, it has been as he understood it.

---

12 Dr. James Evans Rhoads, first president of Bryn Mawr (1885-1894).

13 The New Testament, Romans 6:14-15.

Each student, whatever her gifts, must make it her own if she is ever to be anything but an alien here."

"It always needs Ellen to give the finishing touch," said Edith.

"If it had not been for you and Marjorie," insisted Ellen, "I should still have taken counsel of the cynical outsiders."

"Listen a moment," interrupted Marjorie, "that's it after all."

A band of girls was coming toward them through the moonlight and as they came they sang:

"*Thou Gracious Inspiration, Our Guiding Star,*
Mistress and Mother, All Hail Bryn Mawr."[14]

V

One morning some days later, Ellen was looking out upon a delightful garden in Indianapolis. The day was fine, if warm, and in the garden the roses were in full bloom. She was in the highest spirits; but her gayety of mood was a thing of the past five minutes and had nothing to do with the sunshine or the flowers. She was reviewing the occurrences of the last week and entertaining herself greatly.

Her speech had been made the day before with really brilliant success. It had been the most important event in a series of notable meetings and had been received in a way that might well have roused her to fresh endeavour. Yet in the moment of her greatest success she had shown herself strangely indifferent to her manifest duty. This was the result of her having discovered, just as she had begun to accept the fact of her triumph and the rewards that lay before her, that it was all due to a surprising mishap, something altogether beyond her control. She showed that she felt the importance of the occurrence by thinking of it steadily for the rest of the day and well on into the night. This was not because she wanted to think of it particularly; indeed she had made every effort to dismiss her preoccupation; but she could not rid

---

14 "Thou Gracious Inspiration" was the College hymn before it was replaced by "Sophias." The full lyric goes:

> Thou gracious inspiration, our guiding star,
> Mistress and mother, all hail, Bryn Mawr!
> Goddess of wisdom, thy torch divine
> Doth beacon thy votaries to thy shrine.
> And We, thy daughters, would thy vestals be,
> Thy torch to consecrate eternally.

herself of the idea that an accident was responsible for her triumph. In her perplexity she went over the whole thing time and again.

There had been an inspiring audience, so much she acknowledged, casting her mind over it. She had observed it in the moments before the meeting was called to order. Looking at the impressive throng she had been annoyed to think that she might have to use her notes. As she rose and moved toward the desk there had been a sudden hush and concentration of attention upon the platform, of so much she had been distinctly conscious. She had felt too that after she laid her notes on the table and began to speak, the intelligent interest which had greeted her opening sentences soon gave way to an eager, fixed intentness and breathless silence. Then all was a blank, till the restrained enthusiasm broke forth.

As soon as the meeting was over she had been overwhelmed by congratulations. Her one desire had been to escape, and she felt it difficult to be gracious to her admirers. She had managed at length to get away, and handing her notes to a reporter, had hurried to the door. There she had been stopped by an old gentleman, who, though an utter stranger to her, greeted her as an old friend.

"Now, Miss Blake, you'll come home with us. You'll not stop another minute at the hotel. No, I'll not hear a word. I won't take a refusal. Nobody has as good a right to you as I, your father's old friend, Ned Cartwright." Then he had grasped her warmly by the hand, exclaiming delightedly,—"My dear young lady! My dear young lady! It was your father over again, Harry Blake, Prince Hal we used to call him. And is that the way you girls feel about college? Bless me, I'd never have believed it. I have heard so much solemn nonsense talked about what you do and say and think. But I'll never believe it again. Why, you might have been talking about my own college days, and your father's too,—Prince Hal we used to call him. I'll never forget how we stole the clapper, he and I. And they do it still, my dear, just as we used to, and you steal your clappers too, and, bless me,—I'll send every girl I can to college, if that's the way you all feel about it. That's education! It isn't all books,—never was and never will be. Just ask your father and he'll tell you so too. Yes, I give you my word, every one of them shall go. I'll see to it. I'd as soon shut them off from fairy stories and Walter Scott, and falling in love, because they were girls. It's romance, that's what it is and they've a right to their romance; for I'm an old man, my dear, and perhaps you'll take my word for it, it's the romance of life that counts,—for the girls as well as the boys."

While he was still talking Mrs. Cartwright had come up with a welcome as hearty as his. Their hospitality had been irresistible, and Ellen, powerless before it, was soon walking with them to the carriage. But just as she had been about to get in she had been stopped once more.

"Pardon me, Miss Blake," some one had said, and there had stood the reporter with her manuscript.

"I think there must be some mistake," he had gone on to say, "the paper you gave me deals with the practical value of college life and you talked this morning on what you called 'the Poetry of College Spirit.'"

Then, as in a flash, Ellen had seemed to understand the sense of something strange and bewildering in the experience of the past hour, for she then remembered that when she had stood facing her audience in the moment before she began to speak, she had seemed to forget her notes, her listeners and herself, and to apprehend the meaning of her four years at Bryn Mawr so clearly that it came to have for her a sort of personal identity. Carried beyond herself by her delight in the assurance of something actual, she had spoken unpremeditated thoughts. One might almost say, she thought, that the memories revived by the visit to Bryn Mawr, then crowded out by her intense preoccupation in the business of the convention had, as in revenge, taken possession of her, forcing all other thoughts from her—had almost as it were expressed themselves. Much that had puzzled her in Major Cartwright's criticism was now explained. A trick of memory accounted for all—even her triumph. But she could recall nothing of her speech. The words were forever lost.

She had been overwhelmed by the strangeness of it all, and, do what she would, she could not keep her thoughts from wandering from the Major's eager questions of her father's doings to her own perplexing experience. At one moment she had seemed to be on the point of remembering the speech, to have the words on the tip of her tongue; the next to lose them more surely than ever. Though the Major was constantly bringing it to mind she was none the wiser for his references. That he had thought well of it she could not doubt, but she wanted to know what she had said. Long after she had gone to her room that night she had sat thinking. The poetry of college spirit!

What had she said about it? Perhaps she had said something absurd, had made her subject ridiculous. It hardly seemed so from what she had heard. And yet,—could she think that the inspiration of that moment of discovery had lasted through an hour of unconsciousness? How much more probable that the shadowy something she had tried to define had been so real to the memory or the imagination of her hearers that the mere mention of it had for them an instant fascination.

And now this morning, finding herself the first downstairs, she had picked up the paper. She would find out at last. A few moments ago she had finished reading, and throwing the paper aside with the impatience of disappointment, had stepped out on to the porch. In those five minutes she had come to view the whole thing with a lively enjoyment.

There was a column about it in the paper, but no outline, nothing but praise and the hope that she would make her speech fully effective by publishing it. Was there perhaps a touch of malice in that suggestion? Had the reporter grasped more of the situation than she had chosen to tell? With that thought amusement overpowered her,—amusement at herself above all. That she of all persons should be at a loss to know how she had done precisely what she desired to do—please everybody—seemed to her the perfection of irony. Her comic imagination, once kindled, swept everything before it, her self-importance, her views, even her curiosity. Then a delightful feeling of irresponsibility came upon her. The speech was none of hers.

"Well now, what an early riser you are. I hope you are not used up by the excitement of yesterday," came in cordial tones from the doorway and Major Cartwright came out to bid her good-morning.

"What, all alone!" looking about him. "Haven't you seen Mrs. Cartwright yet? She's been down a long time. I suppose she's out among the roses. We'll go on without her if you don't mind. She likes to take her time and cut all the roses before the sun gets hot, but it worries her to think she is keeping me waiting. So I humour her and myself too."

"Well, you'll not be asked to wait this morning, my dear Edward, I've got them all gathered." And Mrs. Cartwright came up from the garden with a basket of roses on her arm. "Come away to breakfast now. I'll arrange these afterward," leading the way to the dining-room.

The Major picked up the paper in passing, and looked at it.

"Oh here's all about your speech!" he cried, "I hope they didn't garble it very much."

"Far from that," laughed Ellen, "they don't attempt to tell what I said."

"What? You don't mean it. Nothing at all about it?"

"Oh, yes, compliments enough to turn my head. But the thought was evidently too much for——"

"Just listen to this, Lucy!" interrupted the Major after a glance at the criticism. "I don't believe you know what a distinguished young lady we have with us this morning,—'Indianapolis has heard much of the eloquence of Miss Blake, but Indianapolis was not prepared for the glowing words of yesterday.'" He read to Ellen's great amusement. "'It would be folly to attempt an abbreviated report of that splendid piece of oratory. Instead we take pleasure in printing extracts from an article on a more practical phase of college life, confident that any words on woman's education from so able an exponent will be of the highest interest to our readers.

"'The speech made yesterday we predict, without hesitation will never be surpassed by Miss Blake,—it will be remembered as her masterpiece.'"

While he was reading Mrs. Cartwright had been watching Ellen and had decided that she had been blind the night before, for she had missed much of the attraction in her face. Just now Ellen's eyes twinkling with fun were fixed on the major's face, and Mrs. Cartwright watched her with a pleased smile.

"Your masterpiece he calls it," she exclaimed, as her husband finished; "isn't that just like a reporter? How does he know you'll never surpass it?"

"Bless me, I don't see how she could surpass it," ejaculated the Major, "I'll not call the fellow a false prophet yet."

"I don't believe you'll have the chance—ever," retorted Ellen. "I haven't an idea what I said and by the time I make my next speech no one else will remember."

"What do you mean, my dear young lady?" he asked astonished. "It was never in the world extempore."

"That or nothing." And Ellen, sensitive to a genial change in herself, though, perhaps but dimly conscious of it, told the whole story with so keen a relish for the satiric elements in it, that her listeners were delighted. Her unconcern met with no protest from companions too unfamiliar with her ways to reproach her for not being quite herself. Elsewhere she might not have dared to disregard the imperious demands of what was expected of her; but here she was not coerced by any preconceived notions of what she was likely to do.

"And it's all gone from you?" said Mrs. Cartwright.

"Yes, just as completely as if the thing had never happened. It's just as though you had done something very clever in a dream, and found when you tried to do the same thing after you were awake that you had forgotten the most important part of it."

"But the fellow ought to have attended to his business better," said Major Cartwright. "What was he there for if not to report?" He took up the paper again. "The man's a fool. A plea for the higher education!"

"That's what it was meant for," murmured Ellen.

"It converted you, anyway," contended Mrs. Cartwright, nodding at him.

"Never heard anything so absurd," he went on disregarding them. "Where did he get all this stuff about the practical value of the higher education?"

"From me, I am afraid. You see when he found he couldn't have the best, he decided to take the next best, and asked me for the notes of the speech I intended to make. I tried very hard indeed to catch my thoughts about Bryn Mawr and pin them down for inspection as my views on college life. But they escaped me, I'm glad to say."

"I can't believe it of you. Why when you got through you had stirred in me afresh the enthusiasms of years ago."

"That's not so much of a compliment as it seems, my dear," interrupted Mrs. Cartwright. "His enthusiasm on some subjects is perennial. It needs only the word 'college' to set him going. But come along and help me with the roses. If we go on like this, we'll begin to think you just made an ordinary speech after all."

"And I do want to think it my masterpiece," said Ellen, rising to follow her. Then she turned to the Major with a humorous diffidence that hid a feeling too strong to show itself. "Perhaps it is just as well that I have to stand on my attainment. If it were down in black and white some critical person would be sure to discover how much I owe to the eloquent ears of my audience."

Marian T. MacIntosh, '90.

IN MAYTIME

I

Timothy Trask was an eminently correct young man. His dress, his speech, his manners were all the most correct of their kind. If he discovered that anything was the proper thing to do, he always did it, even to the extent of playing very poor golf in an irreproachable pink coat. He was a great lover of the antique, which is in itself a very correct thing to be at the present time, and he possessed a collection of ancient armour, which was hung about on the walls of his wide front hallway, a grim line of swords and battle-axes, and great round shields.

Large as this collection was, in the mind of the fastidious Timothy it was incomplete without a certain Crusader's dagger, exposed to view in a New York dealer's window. Timothy had stood looking at this dagger with longing contemplation, for once unconscious of his pose before the public gaze. His imagination had conjured up an enticing scene in which Timothy Trask figured as the centre of an admiring throng of acquaintances, all watching with breathless eagerness while he told the story of the ancient dagger and pointed out its jewelled hilt and the fine gold chains attached to each end. Then he had counted over his railway stocks, his mortgages and government bonds, and had sadly taken the train back to Philadelphia.

The dagger continued to fill an unobtrusive place in the New York window, and an altogether too prominent place in the mind of poor Timothy. All his antiques grew tiresome and commonplace in comparison with this one little jewelled hilt. At last one evening he decided that he must have it if it ruined him. With a sudden burst of confidence he told the whole story to three friends in his smoking room, and announced his intention of going to New York the next day.

Unlucky confidence for Timothy! A look of subtle meaning passed from one to another of the friends. One of them, in spite of warning glances from the others, picked up a copy of the *Ledger* from the table, and nonchalantly pointed to a full-page account of a May-day fête, reviving the Elizabethan plays and dances, to be given the next day at Bryn Mawr.

"Here's a lot about the learned ladies. Going to give some sort of show or other. Elizabethan! Hm! Reading extracts from history, I suppose, perhaps all dressed up, like a Dickens reading. It says something about 'correct costumes.' I wonder if Tim's cousin is to be in it. Look here, Tim, when are you going to take us out to see that pretty cousin of yours?"

"I have not seen Marion Hall since she was a child, and have no desire to make her acquaintance," said Timothy icily.

Because Timothy was so correct, he particularly detested and disapproved of college girls. They represented to his mind a mixture of spectacled phenomena of learning, and of cheering, basket-ball playing New Women. In either capacity he found them peculiarly objectionable. He often said of them, with a fervent horror he might have expressed towards wild Indians, "I sincerely trust it will never be my misfortune to meet one."

His feeling towards college girls was well known to these friends and it had occurred to one of them that it would be delightful to see Timothy at the May-day festivity, surrounded by hordes of college girls on their native heath. The incongruity of the picture was so pleasing to the others that the idea had been instantly seized upon, and they determined, by some hook or crook to get Timothy to Bryn Mawr.

Now the avowed trip to New York gave them their opportunity. One of them could meet him at the station and manage in some way to lead him astray.

The victim serenely played into their hands. When the conspirators appeared Timothy was just in the agony of trying to hide his nearsightedness and at the same time discover which was his gate. All the officials seemed occupied at that moment, and he had no time to go back to the bureau of information.

"Hello, Jenks, where are you bound for? I have just two minutes. Can you see which is the New York gate?"

"Over there," replied Jenks, unblushingly pointing to the sign "Bryn Mawr special," under which was a hurrying crowd in holiday attire. Timothy noted the throng and bustle of an express, and pushed through the gate just in time to get a seat.

II

"To the May-pole let us on, The time is swift and will be gone!"

The blue sky, the green campus, the laughter, echoing on every side, repeated the invitation of the song, while the sun poured gayly through the windows, and the voices without mingled with those within. A breakfast party was in progress on the fourth floor of Merion. It was not the first time such a function had been held there, but this morning the fantastic costumes of the guests, the piles of gay cheese-cloth heaped in a corner, the swords and plumed caps lying on top of notebooks, gave the party an unusually festive and holiday appearance.

A herald clad in yellow and white, adorned with rampant lions before and behind, was scrambling eggs by the window-sill, and a forester[15] in a brown jerkin was making coffee in one of the egg-shaped coffee-pots so apt to turn upside down when least expected. A marshal had just set fire to her blue and red coat-of-arms, and was kneeling in front of the divan, engaged in carefully pasting on a patch.

Every now and then a knock announced a newcomer whose costume was greeted with laughter and eagerly examined. Presently a forester appeared, in Lincoln green jerkin and smock. Her arms were full of many-coloured banners, which she proceeded to hang out of the window, flaunting an expanse of purple lions and gilded dragons upon the spring breeze. Then she procured a plate of eggs and potatoes, and a cup of coffee, and sat down on the floor.

"We have been indulging in a little archery practice this morning," she said, laughing softly at the remembrance. "It is going to be very picturesque shooting down that avenue of trees, but it is singularly fortunate that the target is safely out of sight!"

"Don't be discouraged! Wait till you hear the heralds striving to sound their horns," said the sword-dancer, who was sitting on a perilous rocking-chair without a back, while her hair was being turned up beneath her collar. "There, listen to them now!"

There came through the open window a feeble noise, ending abruptly in a squeak, followed by shouts of laughter. Looking out they saw a herald standing with her head thrown back and her trumpet

---

[15] Medieval foresters, with authority equal to that of sheriffs, patrolled woodlands for poachers and other criminals.

raised to her lips, her tall, young figure, in its white and yellow, silhouetted against the green campus. A motley but appreciative audience paused in the task of putting up May-pole streamers to applaud her.

While the others were so engaged, the forester came and sat down on the floor by the marshal, and watched her put the finishing touches to the damaged costume.

"Will you do something for me?" she asked, a trifle shyly.

"With pleasure," said the marshal, outlining her coat-of-arms with black paint.

"Don't say you will so quickly. I had a letter from some one, the other day, saying he was coming to May-day. I wrote him that I didn't want him, but—I am afraid he will come anyway, and I don't want to see him."

"Oh!" said the marshal, looking up.

"I can't make up my mind," said the other girl. "I wish I could, but I can't, and I simply won't see him till I do."

"Oh!" said the marshal again. "I suppose you want me to keep him out of your way?"

"If you only would," assented the forester, with a pleading gaze.

"But my dear young innocence, there are going to be a few thousand people here, more or less. How am I to find one unattached young man?"

"Oh, I only mean, in case you happen to hear of his asking for me. People will come to you, you know. Don't have him too much on your mind."

"I will try not to," said the marshal, dryly. "If you will hear my advice, I think you had better see him for yourself, and settle it, yes or no, one way or other."

"You don't know how hard it is," murmured the forester, with a little sigh.

The marshal rose to her feet with a grim expression, which indicated that she would like the chance of settling it. And with an inward remark upon the nuisance of having men mixed up with college functions, she went to the oval mirror and put on her coat-of-arms.

"The rehearsal is at ten," she announced. "Now, please be on time, every one, so that it need not take *quite* the whole morning to form the procession. Don't forget the cloaks for the band, Elizabeth,— and do all of you remember that *no one* is to wear patent leather shoes!"

She seized her marshal's staff and departed.

III

When Timothy arrived at the Bryn Mawr station, that afternoon, he found himself in the centre of a dense crowd, which was surging up the road. He had no liking for crowds, and avoided them on all occasions. It annoyed him intensely to be surrounded by indiscriminate numbers of chattering people, pushing against him, and pressing him along with them. In spite of his efforts to maintain his usual dignified carriage, he was swept along at a fairly rapid pace, through a gateway, and up a long path to the side of a low stone arch; through which appeared a vista of gleaming white road and green trees.

At Haverford when the familiar Cricket Club came in sight, Timothy had come to a sudden realization of the trick his friends had played him. And when every one trooped out of the train at Bryn Mawr, he had decided to yield to curiosity and make the best of a bad situation. But it was in no genial mood that he approached the college. And now he almost wished he had taken the next train back, to vent his anger on those three friends.

He was sandwiched in between two stout ladies, one of whom poked him in the neck with her parasol, while the other explained the details of Mary's costume, just completed the day before, by the maternal sewing-machine. Timothy correctly protected his necktie from the parasol's advances. Taking out his eyeglass, he assumed his most extreme expression of bored indifference, hoping to indicate to every one around him that he, at least, was not here willingly for a day's holiday, and anticipated no diversion whatever from anything forthcoming. The thought of himself, Timothy Trask, inside a woman's college, waiting by the roadside for a circus procession, was enough to make him grit his teeth, and swear at the three idiots who had been instrumental in sending him there.

Suddenly a hush fell upon the expectant crowd. With a blast upon their shining trumpets, eight heralds appeared in Pembroke archway, dressed in white and gold, with the Pembroke coat-of-arms emblazoned upon their breasts. Behind came lumbering along four oxen, great, patient beasts, decked out with leaves and branches, dragging the May-pole. Some mighty forest-giant had been sacrificed to these revels. It was painted white, and festooned with garlands. A line of flower girls trooped along on either side, flowers in their arms, on their short gay-coloured skirts, and adorning their wide hats.

Laughter rippled down the line of spectators, as through the archway came nine donkies, one behind another, solemnly bearing the famous *Nine Worthies* of Old English pageant. Odds, my life, we find ourselves in high company! Here is Julius Cæsar, clad in scarlet, with a truly Roman nose, and behind him King Solomon, in all his purple glory, while Sir Godfrey de Bouillon, that virtuous knight, brings up the rear on a most restive steed. Next, mounted on a high cart, came the maidens of Spring, fighting their old battle with grey-coated Winter. That is right, pelt him with flowers, and cover his snowballs. He has no place to-day.

It seemed as if Pembroke Arch were a gateway to the past, and jovial Old England were pouring through it.

Now came the ring of horses' hoofs upon the stone paving. Make way, there, for Maid Marian, the Queen of the May, with Robin Hood, that gallant and sturdy rogue, riding by her side! There followed all his merry men, come from the shades of Sherwood to join in the revels, for what true yeoman will not trip a measure with a pretty maid, when the sun shines on May-day? Behind came the fool, in motley red and yellow, bells upon his two long ears, bells upon every point of his skirt and cape, bells upon the sceptre which he shook above his head. Happy fool, with light feet and lighter heart! Treading close on his heels the Hobby-horse was showing his paces. For the most part he walked along, sedately enough, saving his breath to curvet and prance, later on, in the *Revesby Sword Plaie.*

With music and laughter the pageant moved on, a train of shepherds with softly bleating sheep, milkmaids, peddlers, ballad-mongers, and last of all, mounted upon a float, a strange company indeed. They were dressed in classic Grecian folds prepared to act in *The Excellent Pastoral of The Arraignment of Paris.* Cupid is proverbially abroad on May-day, but here he stood, in actual guise, and Pan, too, playing his pipes, and stately Minerva, with her snaky shield.

The pageant wound in and out, around the grey stone buildings, a long thread of living colour. Before Timothy well knew what he was doing, he found himself pressing eagerly on with the crowd to the May-pole green. The flower-crowned pole was loosed from behind the patient oxen, and borne upon eager shoulders to the centre of the green. It was raised aloft in the air, tottered for an instant, a great cheer went up, and it sank into its socket. Then struck up the fiddles and pipes, the dancers hastened to their May-poles, and holding aloft the gay streamers began the dance with a bow and a courtesy.

"All fair lasses have lads to attend 'em
    Jolly, brave dancers who can amend 'em."

They wound the coloured ribbons about the four poles, while the rest of the merrymakers danced at will and to the lilt of the gay tunes, in twos and threes, as their fancy led them.

Timothy watched two flower-girls, tripping a measure with a forester, smiling at him over their shoulders, and finally giving him each a hand and dancing away into the crowd. He felt his pulses beat the time as they had never done in a ballroom. It was the open air, and the gay costumes, and the spirit of Old England, which had somehow taken possession of him. Here was nothing but sunshine and feasting and dancing all day; and after sundown, rest under a hawthorne bush. Timothy even longed to give a hand to that dainty shepherdess and join in the dance.

"Come together, come, sweet lass,
    Let us trip it on the grass."

Presently the music ceased and the dancers scattered to their separate plays. Timothy suddenly bethought him of his cousin. For the moment his desire to claim acquaintance with an Old Englander got the better of his hatred of college girls, and he asked one of the nearest groups where he might find Miss Hall. A tall marshal standing near heard the question, and turned around with a start.

"Did you ask for Miss Hall?" she said. "I will be glad to direct you if you will come with me."

Now Timothy was unaccustomed to having young women, with golden hair, and shining, eager eyes, hold out their hands to him, and say, "Come with me!" He was so taken by surprise that with a mumbled, "Much obliged, I'm sure," he followed her meekly through the crowd towards Dalton Hall.

"It is most unusual," he told himself with misgiving, "for her to address me, a complete stranger, in this way. It must be the policy of the college to propitiate outsiders. I wonder if she would do it to every one."

Then, quite irrelevantly, he wondered if he had on his most becoming shape of collar. For some reason he felt very tolerant towards this girl's naïve eagerness.

Presently she turned back to him, and said: "Would you not like to come over here and see *The Ladie of the Maie*? It is such a pretty little play."

"After all," thought Timothy, "no one knows me here."

He followed her submissively to the very front row of spectators, and sat down on the grass, a thing he had not done before for at least ten years. While they watched, the marshal explained that these shepherds and shepherdesses were all grave seniors, and in one more month would be Bachelors of Arts in fur-trimmed hoods. She told him all the old oral jokes, and Timothy, to whom they were quite new, was much diverted. In return he raked up his almost forgotten college tales. They were not new to the marshal, but she appreciated them so sweetly that Timothy thought they must be even more amusing than he had fancied.

The shepherds departed with their flocks of white, softly-bleating sheep, but before the audience had time to wish them back, a gay, rollicking ditty struck up, and the chimney-sweeps came running in, Jack-o'-the-Green leading. They joined hands and danced around him in a circle, still to the same rollicking measure, while Jack-o'-the-Green, peering through his covering of branches and leaves, bowed to each one in turn. The music stopped with a quick chord, the chimney-sweeps dropped to their knees and pointed their brooms at the figure in the middle. Then the music began again, and with their brooms in front of them, they ran out.

Timothy and his guide stood up, and moved onward with the crowd. He began to feel that there was no immediate necessity of finding Marian Hall. He could just as well take a later train back to town. The marshal was very courteous, and he did not wish to appear rude by leaving her too unceremoniously. He even wished something would happen to detain him.

"I want to take you to the *Saint George Plaie*," said his guide. "It is very funny, and the grads. do it with a great deal of spirit."

Timothy's heart beat fast as he suddenly realized that the marshal was purposely lengthening her task, that she was no more anxious to find Miss Hall than he was. Yet she had known him but half an hour! It made him feel strangely humble.

"Do you know," he said, "I have not even been introduced to you?"

"Let me introduce myself," said the girl, gaily. "Sir Marshal, at your service."

"And I am Sir Lancelot," he declared, modestly, "just returned from the Crusades, and glad to be back in merry England."

"Then, fair Sir Knight," said the marshal, "let me guide you to where Saint George is slaying the unbeliever in sport, as you have so often slain him in reality."

With more of such agreeable foolery, they made their way to where Saint George was indeed slaying every one around him, to the diversion of the spectators. For years afterwards the thought of the Dragon, with rainbow snaky locks, writhing in the throes of death, would bring to Timothy a smile of retrospective amusement.

It was a staging fit for *A Midsummer Night's Dream*. Pembroke was in the background, its grey walls overhung with ivy. A green elm spread its branches on one side of the open space, and on the other was a cherry-tree, a mass of pink blossoms, its soft petals carpeting the grass beneath.

There was no further question of finding Marian Hall. Sir Knight and his guide wandered about everywhere, and Timothy's friends would surely have doubted their eyes, could they have seen him taking in everything with the air of a happy child, while he stated his theories on Old English dances, and masques, and costumes.

At last he said: "Where is that fellow, Robin Hood, whom I saw in the procession? He must be shooting his arrows somewhere about the green."

"I believe he is," said the marshal, without enthusiasm, adding to herself, "How vexatious if I cannot keep him away from there. He will see her, of course, and my day's work will have gone for nothing."

"I should like to see him immensely," observed Timothy.

"It is a long walk," objected the marshal.

"Not *too* long, surely," said Timothy, with a glance, adding persuasively, "I should hate to go alone."

"I should hate to have you," cried the marshal, with unmistakable sincerity.

"Ah!" said Timothy, intoxication mounting to his brain. He wanted to grasp some one by the hand and tell him what an altogether pleasing and agreeable world this was. "Ah!" he said again, "we will go together."

The marshal flushed and murmured, "Idiot!" Then she grew pinker than ever with vexation, while Timothy watched her confusion with an agreeable thrill.

"If he *will* go," thought the marshal, "I must certainly go too, to see that he doesn't get within speaking distance."

So they walked on, past Taylor Hall, and across the May-pole green, down to the hill below Radnor, where Robin Hood's men were holding forth. The crowd of people surged and eddied past them. All the wide expanse of campus was covered with moving throngs, and dotted with the brilliant May-day dresses. Banners of purple and gold and crimson were flaming from every window.

"I have stepped right out of America," remarked Timothy. "This place must be rather like a May-day fête, even on ordinary occasions."

"I hope not," thought the marshal, wearily.

"Those grey stone buildings, with all that ivy, are like feudal castles. I should think that the girls wandering about must be rather decorative, if they wear their caps and gowns."

"Thank you," murmured the marshal.

"I feel like a trespasser," continued Timothy. "The place just suits your costumes. We have no business here. Why did you let us in?"

"I don't know what object there would have been in getting it up, if we didn't let you in," said the marshal, striving not to be bored.

Timothy was still in the clouds as they pushed their way into the inner circle of the crowd, just in time for the finish of a bout at quarter-staff between Robin Hood and Little John. Then Robin Hood ran to the top of the hill, and blew a shrill blast upon his horn. A shout answered him, and his band of merry men, all clad in Lincoln green, came pouring over the brow of the hill. Long ago, when Timothy was a child, Robin Hood had been his hero. He had procured a bow and arrow, and was wont to strut about the back-yard, pretending to shoot the dun deer. Here he was face to face with the famous outlaw, and the old glamour gathered about him. After the familiar scene of Little John's christening, the drinking-horns were filled, and the band threw themselves down upon the soft grass, covered with violets. All listened while the minstrel touched his harp, and the beautiful voice of Allan-a-Dale sang the plaintive old ballad *Islington*.

Timothy was still hearing the echoes of the song when his guide said to him, "It is all over. That is the last of the day."

"I should like to see it over again," sighed Timothy.

The girl laughed impatiently. "If you are going back to town to-night, I am afraid you will have to go at once. The train leaves in about ten minutes. Good-night," and she held out her hand to him.

"Good-night," said Timothy. "Do you know," he said, "I have to thank you for one of the pleasantest days of my life."

"I am very glad," said the marshal, not knowing what else to say.

"I am going home to write a love-story," declared Timothy, "all about Old England and May-day, and you shall be the heroine!"

"Thank you very much," said the marshal. "It is getting very late, Sir Knight. I must really say good-bye."

"Good-bye, good-bye, Sir Marshal—till next May-day," cried Timothy. He stood still, looking after her tall, erect figure, as she made her way through the dwindling crowd.

Darkness had fallen quickly, and the space about him was almost deserted. The great grey buildings loomed up dimly in the twilight. A group of girls strolled past him, singing *Islington*, and the wind brought back the sweet, plaintive notes. Timothy still saw beside him the quaint figure of the marshal, the curls flying out from beneath her rounded cap, her eyes looking up at him as she explained the May-day sights and sounds. It seemed hardly possible that she was not a reality, that he could stretch out his hand and not touch her. But he would see her again; Philadelphia and Bryn Mawr were not far apart. The distant train whistled, and gave a few warning puffs, which rapidly increased in number as it drew out of the station. Timothy leaned against a tree and indulged in dreams.

Two foresters were standing near by, talking eagerly. But it was some time before Timothy realized the purport of their words.

"It was the funniest thing you ever heard of," one of them was saying. "Poor Eleanor! I saw her with him some time ago, and now she has just told me what happened. You see I asked her to take care of Jack for me, and keep him from finding me—why, yes, of course I had my reasons—and somehow she got hold of the wrong man. She has kept this creature with her all the afternoon, *all the afternoon*, my dear, thinking he was *Jack*! And she says he is the most awful stick, and has bored her to death, poor dear! Isn't it a joke on her? It is a good joke on me, too, because I was so sure that Jack would come. I wonder why he didn't!"

Lights were beginning to twinkle in the windows. The chorus of *Islington* still came back on the breeze, but it sounded quite different to Timothy. Somehow everything had suddenly become common-place.

"I think," he said, with a deep breath, "it was a pretty good joke on me."

Then he pulled down his hat, buttoned his coat, and set off towards the station, with all possible speed.

Anne Maynard Kidder, 1903.

WITHIN FOUR YEARS

In the dry, warm darkness of a May evening two girls lay on the grass near the tennis-courts north of Taylor. It was in the days when the present athletic field was only a roadway and a damp hollow where dog-tooth violets grew. Radnor and Merion loomed across the campus, their few lighted windows betraying how little the spirit of study possessed the hour. All the light and brilliancy of the college seemed concentrated in Denbigh dining-room, whence, through wide open windows, came the laughter and songs of the supper the juniors were giving the seniors.

There were sound and movement, too, in the obscurity under the windows. Now and then a hand and arm, or a head, rose from the shuffling, murmuring mass, and for a brief moment came into relief against the bright oblong of the window, the hand in its withdrawal seeming always to carry with it something very like a cup or a plate, which was received below with shrieks or even some boldly distinct remarks.

One of the girls on the grass sat up suddenly, a stiffness of disapproval apparent in her attitude, even in the dim light from the library windows.

"That is all a disappointment to me." She supplemented her remark by a quick movement of one arm in the direction of Denbigh.

"Why?" The other girl turned, resting her head on her curved arm.

"To think that college girls can be so frivolous, so silly. It isn't at all what I expected before I came."

"You didn't suppose we talked in Greek all the time, did you, Lilian?"

"Of course I didn't think absurdities, Clara. But I did think college girls would be dignified and serious, and wouldn't act like a rabble of street boys. And *that*, I think is immoral." She rose with her back to Clara, as from Denbigh came, full and strong, reënforced by the voices of the freshmen under the windows, the chorus:

"Then here's to Bryn Mawr College, Drink her down, drink her down——"

Clara West clasped her arms around her knees and rested her cheek on them, murmuring in a sort of ecstasy, "I love it all."

Clara West was a quiet girl with odd impulses. One of these had been to ask Lilian Coles to sit with her for a while on the campus, as they happened to leave the library together. The oddity in this case was not that Clara was a sophomore and Lilian a freshman—class lines were then very loosely drawn. But Lilian was not the sort of girl every one would choose to sit on the grass with under the stars and listen to college songs. Lilian had accepted only because she was waiting for a reference book she wanted. It was this she now went in quest of, after bidding Clara a rather impatient good-night.

As she stopped by the half-open door of one of the first floor studies in Merion, a tall girl with smooth, red-brown hair parted in a straight white line, swung herself around from her desk and smiled.

"Oh, Miss Coles! You have come for the 'Augustan Poets'? I have just finished."

She wore a pretty organdie gown, for she was as scrupulous in maintaining the tradition of dressing for dinner as in every other detail of her well-ordered existence. The study seemed rather bare, but there were a few rich rugs on the floor and on the flat couch, and large photographs of Greek sculptures on the walls. A tea table by the hearth was loaded with cups and saucers, cakes and sandwiches; and thin steam was beginning to come from a kettle hanging on an iron tripod.

"Won't you stay and have some tea?" Edith Dareham asked, as Lilian turned away with the book. "Some of the girls are coming in to talk over our play for the freshmen next fall."

"No, thank you, I don't drink tea, and—I don't believe in plays." With this bomb-like deliverance Lilian disappeared. Edith looked bewildered and rather pained.

"The people evidently don't want your 'panis et circenses,'"[16] mocked a voice close at hand, and a pretty head thrust itself beyond one of the bedroom portières.

"Oh, Blanche dear, are you there? Won't you come out and help me make the tea?"

---

[16] Latin for "bread and circuses."

Lilian hurried out of Merion, meeting groups of freshmen and sophomores. A few of them nodded indifferently to her, but the majority seemed not to heed her. As she crunched over the gravel toward Radnor, where more lights were appearing, she had a sharp feeling of discomfort, unrelieved by any sense of heroism. She was well constituted for martyrdom, but just now the performance of duty seemed a very ungracious task.

Lilian was a victim of a world-old opposition, taking form in her in a conflict between a habit of thought imposed by training, and certain essential, though still latent, qualities of her nature. She was in a stage of intense admiration for Edith Dareham, unconsciously influenced by much in Edith that appealed to the undeveloped side of her character, though attributing her admiration wholly to the obvious traits revealed in Edith's fine conscientious work. Yet she felt an antagonism toward the fact that Edith gave encouragement, or at least tolerance, to certain features of college life that seemed very reprehensible to Lilian, according to the peculiar tenets of the religion in which she had been trained.

Her father was a member of a small religious sect, most numerous in the West, whose creed would seem, to the uninitiated, to be wholly negative, in its exclusion of all that makes for the brightness of life. The sect, though small, was vigorous in proselytism, and Lilian's father had been sent out as a missionary, first to Germany, then to Switzerland. Here had been for Lilian a vast increase in the chances for education; and with a natural aptitude and a child's facility she acquired a good knowledge of French and German. The leaders of this sect had established a small so-called college—really a school for the study of the Bible, with their doctrinal interpretations—because, in the anticipation of an imminent ending of the world, they deemed time too short to be spent on any other line of study.

At about the time of Lilian's return to America, the school had been placed in charge of a man of good academic training, but of a difficult temper that had driven him from place to place till he had accepted this position as almost a last resort. When Lilian was placed in the school he quickly discovered the possibilities of her mind, and for three years gave her a rigorous training. He then advised her father to send her to college. Mr. Coles was not blind to some of the advantages shrewdly presented by the little instructor. He laid the matter before a committee of elders of the society, and consent was finally given. Before her departure, Lilian was called into the presence of the elders, and her opportunities for witnessing to the "light" in a new field, her duty of non-compliance, were solemnly, almost threateningly impressed upon her. The college was chosen by the instructor. The question of money presented difficulties at first, but was finally arranged, and Lilian went on for the examinations with a confidence born of her teacher's encouragement, and justified by her success.

To-night, as she went through Radnor, she could hear laughter, singing, rustling and skurrying,—all the relaxations of a Friday night, with festivity in progress. There was something almost greedy in the haste with which she lighted her lamp, closed her door, and drew down the window shade. Her unworded thought was that others might so waste their time if they chose; she could not afford to. Something of Lilian's reaction to her present environment might have been divined from her face. The forehead was of good shape, but too full for the thin, refined lower features. At her temples the veins were very distinct.

She studied until after the seniors and juniors returned from their supper. Her thoroughness in work was largely temperamental. She still looked upon her opportunities in college simply as means to greater efficiency in the missionary work she had been chosen to do—work that was in fact the propagation of certain peculiar theories. To her simple thinking, it was a sacrifice of herself to make the world better. Her anxiety over the approaching examinations was great.

The next morning she would gladly have gone to the library immediately after breakfast, but it was characteristic of her that she went instead for a two mile walk which she did not in the least enjoy. The Gulph road, behind the college, was a green cathedral aisle, starred with the white flowers of the dogwood. She did not know it. The rhododendrons were in brilliant bloom on the well-kept lawn of a country-place near the pond. She did not see them. But when she came in she was sure that she could not fail on Grimm's law.[17]

Lilian's marks at the mid-year examinations had been good, but not high enough to be striking, and as she left college as soon as the May examinations were finished and thus escaped the inevitable comparing of marks, no one knew how high were the grades she received.

---

[17] A rule in linguistics, describing changes in pronunciation as words from Proto-Indo-European developed into words used in Proto-Germanic.

The excellence of her work, however, unperceived during her first year, save by very few, could not fail of notice as her sophomore year went on, and after the result of the February examination was known, aroused a dim uneasiness among some very devoted friends of Edith Dareham's. The general rough grading of the members of the class during the first year is apt to be accurate, and, with a little shifting, is accepted as permanent in the second year. Edith Dareham was now the recognized European Fellow of the class of '9_.

"You don't suppose there is any danger, do you?" was the query put to a group in a cozy Denbigh study one February afternoon before dinner. It was growing dark with a gathering storm, and the wind was whirling clouds of snow across the campus. In the room the gas was lighted, a coal fire was glowing in the grate, and two alcohol lamps were steadily burning. The querist was Katherine Leonard, "a junior by courtesy," she frankly qualified herself. Indeed a degree for her did seem at least problematical, not so much through neglect of hard work as through a perverse inclination to interest herself ardently in courses of reading quite foreign to her majors. She was absorbed in literature and philosophy while painfully struggling with mathematics and physics, and as these latter subjects scarcely permit a divided allegiance even to minds most gifted in that direction, the issue threatened to be disastrous for Katherine. But when urged to change her majors she simply shook her head. She needed the discipline, she said.

"Danger of what?" demanded Blanche Merrill, Edith Dareham's roommate, with an abrupt turn to Katherine.

"That Lilian Coles may take the fellowship from Edith."

"Of course not! How absurd!" replied Blanche superbly.

"Don't be too sure, Blanchette, dear," interposed a tall girl who was writing at a table under the gas. She was copying a lecture from her hostess's notebook into her own, and kept on while she was talking.

"Don't use that absurd name, Clothilde, any one would think I was a Trouville donkey.[18] You might as well say 'Papillon.'"

"Thank you, I will. But *revenons*[19]—the fellowships are very uncertain certainties, and who can say what will happen with a girl who gets high credit in the gym."

---

[18] At Trouville, a popular tourist location in Normandy, there have been donkey races for many years.

"Then Edith may as well give up." Katherine's small form yielded to a spasm of laughter at the recollection of Edith's doing two hours a day in the gymnasium in order to avoid a condition.

"Yes," commented Blanche, "when Edith went to the gym before breakfast, Katherine would go and hold Thucydides up before her, so that Edith could put a last polish on her translation while she was doing chest weights and quarter circle."

"That isn't really true, you know," Katherine coolly joined in the laughter of the others. "That is, it's true only to the spirit, not to the fact. I would have done it if it had been necessary. But really it would be unjust to the college to give the fellowship to a girl who won't go to a tea."

"Is Miss Leonard here?" In response to a low rap some one had opened the door to Lilian Coles who stood a little bewildered at the contrast between the still unlighted hall and the bright room. Katherine freed herself from the group on the floor.

"Oh, you have brought that book. I wish you hadn't. I'll have to read it now. Come up, and I will give you the other. I haven't read it. I have been skating all the afternoon. Mabel, please hand me my skates."

"Won't you come in and have a cup of cocoa? It is so cold outside," Lilian was temptingly urged by the fair-haired girl who was nominally mistress of the study, though both she and her roommate were usually obliged to work in the library, so thoroughly did a reputation for hospitality characterize their room. Lilian wanted to go in, but without hesitation declined and started away with Katherine.

"Wait a moment," Katherine touched Lilian's arm and turned back to the open door. Two girls had begun to sing, in response to the guitar of a third,

"Drink to me only with thine eyes."

While Katherine listened to the song, Lilian's eyes rested curiously first on the sensitive face, then on the black sweater, short corduroy skirt and heavy boots that made up Katherine's skating costume.

"I am glad I am not so conscientious as Helen Arnold," Katherine said, at the close of the song. "When her aunt wanted to take her to Bayreuth last summer, she wouldn't go, because, not having an intellectual appreciation of music, she couldn't, forsooth, permit herself

---

[19] French imperative, "let us come back" (e.g., to the subject at hand).

so much emotional enjoyment." Lilian looked puzzled yet stern. She could not but approve the action, though the motive seemed to her unnecessarily refined.

Katherine's rooms were on the second floor. When the two girls entered, the study was in the shadowy dimness of grey twilight cheered by a warm fire. Katherine lighted an old Venetian lantern and some red-shaded candles, then drew the sash curtains which were of dark red silk with arabesques of fine gold lines. Above the mantel hung two carbon photographs of Fra Angelico angels in vellum frames; and at one end stood a bronze of the Flying Mercury, at the other a cast of the Olympian Hermes. On the walls were photographs of Matthew Arnold,[20] Christina Rossetti,[21] and Cardinal Newman[22]; also some prints that Katherine fondly believed to be original Dürers. These objects had not the interpretative value for Lilian that they might have had for another; but the whole suggested luxury to her, and her eyes turned away disapprovingly to fall with a sort of startled horror on the recess left between two bookcases, where, against a dark background, hung an exquisite ivory crucifix. Lilian's attitude toward Catholicism was of the original Puritan inflexibility, strengthened by the exaggerated hatred of the class of people among whom she had lived. And she knew nothing of any concessions due to the opinions of others. The crucifix represented merely a sympathy, not a tendency on Katherine's part. But this fact, even if it had been known to Lilian, would have served none the less to intensify in her a feeling of radical difference between Katherine's governing ideals and her own.

When she entered Radnor on her return, two girls were coming slowly down the stairs, absorbed in confidential chat. They smiled at Lilian as she passed, but she knew that she had no share in the friendship expressed even by the touch of Clara's hand on Ethel's shoulder. She drew herself up sharply, remembering her longing to enter Florence Baker's bright, gay study.

---

[20] British poet and critic (1822-1888) with unorthodox religious opinions, he approached religion as an aesthetic experience.

[21] English poet (1830-1894) who wrote devotional and other verse, and frequently a model for the artist Dante Rossetti, her brother; she sat as the model for the Virgin Mary in his first completed oil.

[22] Cardinal John Henry Newman (1801-1890), a British convert to Catholicism who wrote voluminously and worked ceaselessly for Catholic higher education.

Her way to her room took her past the single suites. The door of one was open, and within were trunks and signs of packing.

"Are you going away?" she paused to ask. Gertrude Elbridge, a pretty little freshman, came forward and drooped against the door.

"Yes, you know I have been ill since the examinations, and papa has sent for me."

"I am sorry." This was true, as Lilian had a mild fondness for the child, despite the fact that, through evenings of loud and prolonged hilarity, Gertrude and her friends had made life a burden to Lilian, and with direct consequence, to the members of the Executive Board of Self-Government. Lilian went on to her room, indignation possessing her. She knew why Gertrude was going away. Before each examination Gertrude had studied all night, her head bound in a wet towel. The towel really bothered her, but she knew that was what her brother did. She had kept awake on strong tea and coffee supplied by sympathizing friends. But evidently even these frantic efforts had not proved redemptive.

"Why," Lilian asked herself, "did not the stronger girls of the college bring a pressure of sentiment to bear against these follies, instead of encouraging them by their own customs?" Was it not her duty to make some protest? An unavailing one it would doubtless be, but surely it is only a lukewarm reformer that considers results rather than principles.

She had returned to college in the fall with a strengthened antagonism to what her father called the worldliness of college life. His influence was still dominant with her. His vision was crude, and he denounced, with a solemnity appealing to the girl's native earnestness, all the joyous innocent froth of amusement that danced over the current of the real, serious life of the college.

In truth, Lilian had departed further from her father's beliefs than she realized. She had already gained an historical perspective and a certain habit of cool unbiased judgment that were forcing her to see in what ignorance and narrowness of mind those beliefs were conceived and accepted. At the same time the studies that had modified her views, tended to increase her sense of the preciousness of time, of the seriousness of life. Her loyalty to her father's teachings was stirred by an unanalyzed appreciation of the change in herself. And now, in the failure of Gertrude Elbridge she seemed to find a justification of the rigidly prohibitive lines her father would throw around all conduct.

She could not see, yet, that the weak have their hard lessons to learn in the opportunities of the strong.

Unfortunately opportunity was not lacking Lilian Coles for that word of protest she felt bound to utter. She always attended the Sunday evening meetings, though little in sympathy with their spirit. The next Sunday she went early. Into the dimly lighted gymnasium came the girls, eyes sparkling and cheeks red from the clear cold air without. Nearly all were wrapped in shawls, but one girl wore a hat and coat and carried a bag. There was a big bunch of violets on the lapel of her coat, and she smiled rather consciously at some comments of the girls she joined. In the first row of chairs were some dignified seniors whom Lilian rather feared, and a junior who at once attracted and repelled her. She was, in spite of herself, fascinated by a cleverness that manifested itself in every department of the college, that would be a force in literature some day, so every one said; and at the same time she had a feeling that there was nothing the girl would not sacrifice to ambition.

At last Helen Arnold, who was to lead the meeting, came in accompanied by Edith Dareham. Helen was the girl who had refused to go to Bayreuth. She busied herself with great care in arranging the books and lamp on a little table. Her friends knew that she was embarrassed. She was a frail-looking girl, one who set a high value on things that were still unapprehended by Lilian, in their real nature.

She began with a short quotation and took, as a point of departure, the lines:
"That thread of the all-sustaining beauty
   Which runs through all and doth all unite."[23]

With well-chosen words she modestly brought out her thought of the duty of each one to seek for this thread of beauty in all things. Then she spoke, with a little more insistence, of the beautiful in art and in nature, which, she believed, demanded for its true appreciation the highest cultivation not only of mind and age, but of soul as well.

After a short silence, Elizabeth Carrington, Helen's roommate, spoke, weaving Helen's thought into the larger one of that endeavor toward perfection sacredly enjoined upon us. With an impatience

---

[23] From James Russell Lowell's poem, "The Vision of Sir Launfall," first published in 1848. These lines are from the sixth and final stanza to Part First, and at one time were often quoted to encourage heartfelt charity to the needy.

born of the incomprehension of her mood, Lilian had listened to
Helen. She did not hear Elizabeth, who had scarcely finished speaking, when Lilian rose. The girls looked surprised; but after the conse-
crated formula—"It seems to me"—various expressions replaced the
surprise. Some of the listeners looked coldly bored or contemptuous,
a few were amused, but the majority sat ill at ease with pained faces.
Lilian was arraigning them for so much time spent in idle conversation, and in "feasting"—she fiercely put it. She denounced them for
their plays, their dancing. In her excitement she assumed the tone and
phraseology of the denunciations she had been accustomed to hear
from childhood and she went farther than she intended. She said their
pursuit of knowledge was only for its vain shows. The nature of the
silence into which her words fell should have warned her, but some
confused association of ideas carried her on to a bitter allusion to Catholicism. She was recalled to herself by the indignant protest on Hel-
en's face. Clothilde and one or two others present were Catholics.
Lilian choked and stopped.

"Shall we not sing?" suggested Helen. Clothilde started the hymn.
There was no more speaking. Lilian was the first to leave the meeting.
She went out with unseeing eyes and hot cheeks, alone. There are
times when even the kindest hearts are cold, and for the moment
there could be nothing but alienation from one who had found tongue
against the college spirit—for they felt that the attack was really against
this vague, shadowy, stern, beloved thing of many hues and many
forms—the spirit of the college.

Outside, the moon had risen in a clear star-powdered sky, and
was silvering the crusted snow and the ice sheaths that rain and frost
had left on every twig and branch of the trees. The sparkle and splendour of the night only smote Lilian as a part of that whole body of
beauty which, it seemed to her excited thinking, had been presented
that evening as of equal importance with goodness and morality.

There is little tea drinking on Sunday evening. Many girls are
away. It is the time for writing home letters, or doing a little quiet reading. The rooms never seem so warm or the lights so bright as on other
nights. The halls are still and everybody goes to bed early. But this
night there was a little more excitement as girls stopped to talk with
indignation, amusement or indifference of Lilian's outburst. Katherine
Leonard found several girls in Edith's room when she stopped, after

an errand in Radnor. She sought each face questioningly, then dropped on the couch. "How awfully *funny*—how dreadful it was!"

"I can't understand the state of mind that would lead to that," said Alice Warburton. "Where has such narrow-minded egotism been fostered? Such injustice! What an arid life she must have known."

"I admire her!" said Elizabeth Carrington decisively. "I was near enough to her to-night to see how tightly she clung to the chair in front of her. Her knuckles were all white and shiny. It was real heroism. I doubt if any one of us will ever show as much."

"I should hope not!" Blanche commented energetically.

There was a girl lying on the couch who had been reading *Diana of the Crossways*,[24] all this time. She occasionally made notes on the margins. Now she looked up. "For my part, I prefer goodness to cleverness," was all she said. Then she went on reading again. The girls all laughed a good deal. Then there was silence, and some of them laughed again—a little. Some of them were very much of Lilian Coles' opinion in regard to this girl, who was the junior Lilian had noticed in the gymnasium.

"She has greatly relieved my mind, at any rate," said Katherine. "She can never hope for the fellowship now."

"You have no right to say that." Edith was a little sharp. She was somewhat troubled within herself. She liked the serene state of mind that her usual conduct of life granted her, and hated a mean feeling with an intensification of the disgust that any contact with uncleanness gave to her physical fastidiousness. In the dissatisfaction that she had occasionally felt of late, it had occurred to her that she might settle issues with herself by some plan involving sacrifice on her part. But injustice was no dearer to her than selfishness. She fell asleep that night with the healthy resolve not to be troubled by what she could not help.

Meanwhile Lilian Coles was lying on her bed, in the dark, with wide-open eyes. She was restless with a shamed sense that she had violated her finest instincts. She continually wondered how she *could* have done such a thing. Then all the questionings that had been forming in her deeper consciousness for nearly two years, came forward,

---

[24] George Meredith's 1885 novel, which deals with the travails of a highly intelligent, strong woman trying to make her mark in mid-19th century England, despite her miserable marriage.

insisting on a hearing. Helen Arnold's talk that evening passed through her mind with a new meaning and force, but she was too much exhausted then to come to any conclusions. She finally fell asleep, hoping that every one would be too busy to remember her speech very long.

One Saturday morning in the spring Lilian started downstairs. It was late, she was tired and vexed at her slothfulness. She had gone to bed the night before so tired that one night's rest was wholly insufficient. As she reached the foot of the stairs a girl came out of the bathroom with a kettle of water. She nodded to Lilian, went on, then turned.

"Miss Coles, you are sure not to find anything hot for breakfast. Won't you come into my room? We are going to have breakfast there."

Lilian hesitated. Something, perhaps an animating suggestiveness in the spring air that was sweeping through the windows, perhaps the mere yielding of tired flesh to kindly human influences, moved her to accept.

Hester Grey's room looked over the fields and low hills. Two study tables had been put together and were covered with white embroidered cloths. A bowl of violets was on one table and a dish of strawberries on the other, while the more substantial provisions for the breakfast were on a side-table. This separation was due to an arbitrary distinction of Hester's, food taking precedence in her ideas according to its appeal to the eye.

There were two girls in the window-seat and another in a steamer-chair. This one sprang up and insisted on giving Lilian the chair, tucking the pillow behind her with an unceremonious friendliness very grateful to Lilian.

Then she began cutting bread, urging that some one else pass Lilian the olives.

"Do you think you will want more sugar in your cocoa?" Hester asked Lilian. "Of course she will," said one of the girls in the window, without looking up from her book. "You never make it sweet enough." Lilian thought this was very rude, but Hester didn't seem to notice it. She carried a cup to Lilian, who looked at her curiously. Lilian had always had a thought of scorn in her opinion of this girl, whose erratic work, spasmodic brilliancy and general idleness were known to the whole college. Lilian knew that she would sit for hours on the stone wall of the Harriton burying ground doing nothing, even if examinations began the next day. No one ever seemed to be able to foretell whether she would get High Credit or a condition in any examination. Lilian had seen her absorbed in *Treasure Island* the day before the English essays were due. Hester's essay on Keats was written in one night, so rumour said. It received the only High Credit. Lilian had read it, with something like astonishment at the feeling aroused in herself by the revelation of another girl's mind. She had come to have a feeling like reverence for this girl, realizing at last that some gifts of the spirit are not to be measured by so many hours of study, so many hours of exercise. And now this same girl was apparently concentrating her whole mind on the amount of sugar to be added to each cup.

Then Lilian had to think a little about the other girls in the room. They had always seemed to her commonplace, doing but indifferent work. At least they had won no distinction. She knew that the five were close friends, that they couldn't have the fullest enjoyment with her in the room, yet they were unaffectedly genial and hospitable to her. While she, with a perversity which shocked her, did not care if they did enjoy themselves a little less on her account. She wanted what they were giving her.

It is a truism that some actions most important to ourselves or others often seem but pure whim. Hester could have given no reason—in fact, it was not her habit to await reasons—for asking Lilian Coles to take a walk with her that morning. And Lilian, to whom even tying her shoe was often occasion for a mental inquisition, did not care to explain to herself why she accepted the invitation with eagerness. She had intended to spend the morning in making a tabulation and synopsis of some second year English reading. But the pain of that unforgettable Sunday evening had wrought in Lilian a distrust of her own valuations, and she went with Hester willingly.

The morning freshness was still in the air. Hester took Lilian through the woods where the starting leaves wreathed the grey tree-trunks and slim branches like trails of green smoke; to a wide bed of spring beauties; past the pond fringed with willows; across the fields to a stream that flung itself over the rocks with a sparkling abandon to the joy of spring. Lilian saw all these things; and she saw, too, the contrast between the rich black of new ploughed fields and the vivid green of winter wheat. She heard a bluebird singing above them. They went on to an old ruined mill, shadowed by tall dark pines whose roots were washed by a wide, shallow creek. Across the stream, there were woods. Here the girls sat under the pines and Hester read aloud from *Undine*.[25] Gradually the wash and splash of the creek were transferred from Lilian's outward to her inward hearing and seemed to be singing to her of a spirit that was in the water. Suddenly she had a vision of the meaning of the old pagan ideals. She lay back on the grass and let her eyes look very far into the blue above the pines. It occurred to her that she would take some books home in vacation and read all the poems noted on the margins of her Horace. She understood now, she thought, something of the delight in that year's work which all the others in the class had expressed and which she had, in some way, missed.

They stopped to rest again on the stone wall of the old burying ground in the woods, and Hester read from Chaucer following her own liking wholly. Lilian went back to her room with a new sense of the beauty of nature, and of the dignity of free, wholesome joyous human life.

There was no time before luncheon for the intended tabulation of ballad poetry, and in the afternoon she turned at once to the assigned reading in Wordsworth and Coleridge. Before coming to college Lilian had been allowed to read very little. Even her study of the Bible had been scarcely more than a search for texts and illustrations in support of the beliefs of her sect. All through this year the reading presented to her had been stimulating her imagination and perception. But partly from habit and partly from the fact of having detected a pleasure in the exercise of these faculties, she had continued to read mechanically and blindly. Now for the first time she permitted herself to read with something more than a desire to go over so many pages in a given time. As she finished the *Hymn of Chamouni*[26] she caught her breath as one whose spirit has been lifted to an unknown height.

The twofold process of growth, of putting off the old and acquiring the new went on in Lilian with alternations of pain and pleasure,

---

[25] In the world of nature magic, an undine is an elemental spirit associated with water. The literary work mentioned here is likely the 1811 novella by Friedrich de la Motte Fouqué, although it could be a reference to "Ondine," the 1842 poem by Aloysius Bertrand.

[26] That is, "Hymn before Sun-rise, in the Vale of Chamouni," a poem by Samuel Taylor Coleridge (1772-1834).

the latter increasingly predominating. When she entered college and for sometime after, she had her father's contempt for what he called "mere learning." But she was led to a very different way of thinking by a better understanding of what scholarship means—of its untiring zeal and care for truth, and of its outlook beyond the fact to the including law. She even came to accept an opinion that, later on, she found thus expressed: "... our deeper curiosity. There is a sense in which it is all superfluous. Its immediate results seem but vanity. One could surely live without them; yet for the future, and for the spiritual life of mankind, these results are destined to become of vast import."[27] Lilian's nature was such, however, that she must always care chiefly for the immediate practical application of the idea.

During her junior year she did some elective work in sociology which completely revised her ideas of philanthropy. She saw how very inadequate were the measures that she had once thought essential to doing good in the world. Her hope of being a missionary was too much a part of herself to be given up easily, yet she knew that she could not represent her former views. She became greatly interested in college settlement work but she found no time to give to it, for she gave to tutoring all the time that she could spare from her regular work. The mental submission and the claim upon her future involved in the arrangement by which her expenses were paid had become impossible to her, and she wished to become self-supporting as soon as possible.

One Saturday morning she was sitting in the biological laboratory, carefully correcting her drawings of nitella, when Miss Hardy, a graduate student with whom she had done some work in sociology, came in and bent over her.

"Should you not like to go into town with me this evening to one of the social meetings of a working-girls' club which has been organized recently? I think you would be interested."

After a moment's thought Lilian decided to go. A girl whom she tutored every Saturday afternoon was ill and that time could be given to the usual Saturday evening work.

When they reached the Broad Street Station, Lilian was surprised to find Helen Arnold, who had been spending the afternoon in town,

---

[27] A passage from the introductory chapter of Josiah Royce's 1892 book, *The Spirit of Modern Philosophy* (Boston: Houghton Mifflin), p. 8.

waiting for them. The clubhouse was in the lower part of the city. After their arrival there, Lilian spent an hour in eager inspection of the
small library, the schedule of classes, and the furnishings of the
rooms. Helen had disappeared. Lilian asked for her, and Miss Hardy
explained, "She comes every Saturday if she can find any one to go to
and from the station with her. She is teaching two or three girls who
can have better positions as soon as they can write and spell better.
This is the only time they have."

Then they went into a large, brightly-lighted room with a waxed
floor. There was a piano at one end, and some one was beginning to
play. The girls, most of them neatly and prettily dressed, were gathered near the piano, while a few young men, with very smooth hair
and rather conspicuous ties, stood in stiff self-consciousness near the
door.

"Young men of good character are invited in once a month,"
whispered Miss Hardy.

A half-grown girl, in heavy shoes, a crumpled red dress, with a
soiled ribbon knotted around her neck, crossed the room and stood
in front of Lilian. Her open scrutiny was beginning to be embarrassing
when Helen came in. She touched the girl on the arm, and was soon
leading the clumsy shoes lightly through a waltz. After two or three
turns Helen sought some one else, and the girl returned to Lilian.

"Say, ain't she sweet?" she said, looking after Helen with eager
eyes. "She teaches somethin' here, and I'm go'ne to learn it. And I
want some white ties like she wears."

It was still early when they started for the station, but on the
streets Lilian saw one or two things that made her glad to think of the
many girls they had left in the simple pleasures of the carefully-
guarded clubrooms.

A slight delay caused them to miss their train, and they had to
spend half an hour in the waiting-room. Miss Hardy found some
evening papers. Helen declined the one offered her, and drew a book
from her shopping-bag.

"What reading is this, Helen?" Miss Hardy laughingly ques-
tioned. Helen blushed a little. "It is really only the third." On the train
the book happened to lie for a moment in Lilian's lap. She noted the

title. It was *Marius, the Epicurean*,[28] and at her earliest opportunity she procured the book and read it.

She read it with intense interest. Here were a care for life—for its pleasures—and a consecration of time that found no necessary detail too small for perfection. The charm of the book was upon her—its flawless form, its sanity, its strenuousness. There was something of the old defiance in her attitude toward this epicureanism, though the character of it was so exalted and pure. But at the close, when Marius simply puts himself aside and accepts death that his dear friend may live—happy in a love denied Marius—she put the book down very softly. By the profound stirring of her sympathies she felt how absolute was her acceptance of the whole character—as consistent with itself in sacrifice as in æsthetic enjoyment.

The constantly increasing deference given Lilian because of the quality of her work contributed much to her contentment. The freer play of her intelligence was making itself felt. By the beginning of their senior year Lilian Coles and Edith Dareham were undoubted rivals for the European Fellowship. But the real excitement over the fellowship was not apparent until after the mid-year examinations. Then the strain began to be wearing on the two girls and their friends.

"I wish the Faculty would come to a decision," said Katherine Leonard one evening in Clothilde Barry's room. She was on the window-seat between a big palm and a pile of notebooks. "If they don't very soon, I'll not get a degree in June. I love this place but I don't want to stay here all my life. It would be hard to fix my affections on another class. But I can't study till I know."

"I think that possibility would stimulate them, if they only knew—" began Blanche.

Just then the door was flung open and Alice Warburton came in impetuously—her usual manner, but some dramatic quality in this present haste must have made itself apparent, for the other girls assailed her breathless silence with questions. What she finally said was: "There is a Faculty meeting in Taylor." After a moment of comprehending silence, Blanche went out quickly. Katherine followed her.

---

[28] *Marius the Epicurean: His Sensations and Ideas*, a novel by Walter Pater, published 1885. The protagonist is a young man living in second century Rome, and the novel explores his intellectual and moral development in an era of change and uncertainty.

"Blanche, if you find out before the doors are locked, won't you come and tell me?"

"I don't know how it will be." Blanche looked anxious and wouldn't stop. Katherine went back to Clothilde's room, and after she had tipped over the palm and broken the jardinière was advised by Clothilde to go home and go to bed. In her own room she took a physics laboratory book and made a feeble attempt to put order into its chaos, but only succeeded in dropping ink over two important calculations. Then she took down a volume of Mazzini's writings in which she had lately become much interested. At the end of half an hour she became aware that she had not turned a page. She left her room and went down to the parlour. All the lights were out, even in the rooms. Over in Taylor there was a dim light in a second floor window. It had no connection with the Faculty meeting, but she chose to consider that it had, and crouched, shivering, in the window until it went out. Then she went stiffly to bed and slept badly. The next morning Blanche came to her soon after breakfast. "Edith wants to see you."

"Oh, Blanche?" But Blanche was already backing out of the door. "I can't tell you anything. Edith hasn't told me anything." Every line of her face was non-committal.

Edith was sitting at her desk writing when Katherine entered. She looked over her shoulder and smiled, but she was very grave. "I have it, Katherine."

Katherine sat down on the window-seat, and bending over pressed her forehead down on Edith's shoulder. Edith turned about and lifted Katherine's face. She was crying—Katherine, in whom the repressions of stoicism had been the least fleeting of many moods. After a while Katherine said, "We were afraid at one time, Blanche and I—that you might do something—rash." It was not necessary for Edith to ask what she meant. She hesitated before speaking. "I have felt troubled. It isn't reasonable, but I haven't been able to get rid of an uncomfortable feeling about Lilian Coles. I *could* go to Europe without the fellowship, and I suppose she can't. But—I wanted it. I did try to think of some way of helping her when I heard last year that there was danger of her having to leave college. But even if I had had the money—that's a sort of thing it is almost impossible to do. It might have seemed a generous thing for me to let my work go a little, but I could not be sure that she wouldn't do better than even my best.

And," Edith gripped the desk hard, "it would have seemed to me a simply wicked sentimentalism to do poor work deliberately for any reason whatever."

Katherine released the sleeve of Edith's gown that she had held crumpled in her hand. "I am so glad you felt just that way."

Blanche came in then to gather up her notebooks.

"How did you find it out, Blanche?" Katherine asked.

"Oh. I found the note under her door when I came down from Ethel's room last night"—Ethel was Blanche's sister—a freshman. "We had been sitting up watching. But Edith was sleeping like a baby. I lit a candle and roused her and gave her the note. I must say she was rather excited until she got the note open and read it." Blanche stopped.

"Did she tell you then?" prompted Katherine.

"She hasn't told me yet. That honour was reserved for you. She lay down again and I kissed her and covered her up and told her to be a good fellow. Then she laughed and so did I, as silly as two loons. She went to sleep. I went upstairs and awakened Helen and Elizabeth. I did not tell them anything, but they understood, and we talked until two in the morning. Imagine Elizabeth and Helen sitting up till two!"

Katherine was popular enough in college, but that did not account for the way numerous groups, from seniors to mid-year freshmen, obstructed her going from Merion to her own room, and thence to Taylor. They asked her unimportant questions, and eyed her curiously. Her face was impassive. The chapel was unusually full. Edith's friends had gathered around her in her usual seat, well forward.

"But that doesn't mean anything," whispered a high freshman voice, "they'd be there just the same anyway."

Lilian's chief supporters were among the graduate students. Those from other colleges looked rather defiant. A few members of the Faculty came in and sat in the back seats. After the short exercises, the announcement was very quickly made. During the storm of applause that greeted Edith's name Lilian sat apparently unmoved. Her hands were very cold, but no one knew that. And no one would ever know how much she had wanted that fellowship. She had been having a very bad quarter of an hour since Clara West, who was back as a graduate student in Greek, managed to find out and let her know that the decision had been made. Three times before, Lilian had heard a similar announcement made, and each time she had thought that the applause would have been just as loud if the other possible girl had been named. Now she knew that there would not have been the same gladness on the faces or the same heartiness in the hand-clappings if she had been the one instead of Edith. She could have made more friends, she believed, but she had thought that she knew a better use for her time. A keen heart-longing was mingled with her disappointment.

A few weeks later the presence of the students in chapel was again specially requested, and more announcements were made, among them, that the Fellowship in History had been given to Lilian Coles.

"I am so glad!" repeated Clara West that evening, strolling with Lilian about the campus. That Lilian was strolling was not without its significance. It was a misty evening after a rainy day. All about them were the tender, yet vivid, colours of early spring—the fields beyond the edge of the campus, and the distant uplands, were veiled in green mist. Near Taylor the Judas-tree was in purple bloom, and further away the Japanese cherries lifted pink sprays against a soft grey sky. Lilian was moved to an appreciation that did not exclude a quality the picture received from the dignity of the buildings, or even from the well-kept condition of turf and walks. She turned to Clara. "No one can ever know," she said, "how glad I am to come back."

It was the day before commencement. Lilian Coles was in the library, selecting some books to take away for the summer. She went to a window that looked toward Rosemont and Villa Nova. She had come to have a sense of wide distances from this window. For the moment, with a swift, scarcely-conscious recognition of new ideals, new standards of life, she felt in herself something of the triumphant onward rush of the Winged Victory dominating this end of the library. This morning the sky was deep blue with a few white clouds. The air was fresh, the trees and grass very green. The slope beyond the tennis-courts was white with daisies. Some professors, in white flannels, were playing tennis on the nearest courts. Girls in white duck or fluffy muslins were moving toward the gymnasium. The college breakfast was to be there at twelve o'clock. Lilian was going. She had refused all invitations until her examinations were over. Then she went to several teas, to a picnic luncheon and to the class supper. She intended to go to the alumnæ banquet Thursday evening.

Lilian found her place at one of the long tables in the gymnasium beside Clara West and opposite Hester Grey. The balustrade of the running-track had been transformed into a frieze of mountain laurel. Laurel and ferns decorated the tables.

The breakfast was nearly over, and the black waiters were serving the ices.

"Can you see Lilian Coles?" Blanche bent around an intervening neighbour to ask Katherine. Katherine, happy in the fact that she would get a degree on the morrow, looked across the tables just as Lilian touched glasses with a freshman, her lips moving in the chorus,

"Here's to Bryn Mawr College!"

It was Hester Grey who saw a solemn look on Lilian's face as they rose to join in "Manus Bryn Mawrensium." But at that moment it seemed to Lilian herself, that of all the "lætissimæ puellæ"[29] she, in her way, was the most joyful.

Elva Lee, '93.

---

[29] Latin that can be rendered as "joyful girls" or "merry maids."

FREE AMONG THE DEAD

I

A quick step came down the hall and stopped. There was a rustle of silk; the step died away in the direction from which it came. Esther raised her head, carefully laying her little clay tablet on its bed of jeweller's cotton as she wheeled around an instant to smile:

"They're a bit shy of us to-night, Sydney. Haven't you finished with Marius?"[30]

Sydney Lodge, who had swung round also and met her eye, answered:

"No wonder they are; I know I'm shy of myself. If only for once we lived in Denbigh! Then we might at least see the Faculty coming down past the staircase window and the lights going out in Taylor and know when the meeting was over." The castors complained as she pushed back her chair, then the sash went up and the breath of the night that came in and rattled Esther's papers tasted like deep well water, wonderfully pure and cool and dark. Esther wrapped her gown about her, for since dinner she had been working in the library, and crossing the study with the very light step of a very strong person leaned out the window behind her friend.

There was no moon, and the enormous star-sown hemisphere whose horizon fell below their feet, was tonight a faint blur of pearl-grey. Almost as faint and illusory was the ground, and the other halls were denoted by pinkish spots and splashes. From many of these, and in especial from the great windows of the library, ran bands of moon-light-coloured light, like a search-light seen transversely, but filmier. A step rang along the board walk, crunched the gravel, dying away muffled and uneven on grass; voices blew up to them from somewhere and a far-off singing that sounded sweet. Sydney Lodge shivered a little and was drawn in to the fire.

---

30 This is another reference to Walter Pater's 1885 novel, *Marius the Epicurean*, which was mentioned in the preceding story in this collection.

"Lie down and scorch your fuzzy head, young Shelley. The ten o'clock bell hasn't rung and they won't agree for hours yet."

"They never take long over the graduate fellowships,—they put them off, as last year; still, I admit the senior one is hard to settle," acknowledged Sydney, mischievously.

Esther answered with joyful appreciation: "This is quite the most picturesque situation we were ever in. If you don't get it I shall be comforted by its being Hilda——"

"—and if Hilda misses it we've all three the satisfaction of knowing the honour is yours—all three, mark you; for it is an honour, you know. And one of us must get it," finished Sydney with conviction.

At the door a knock made both girls turn pale, but as it opened appeared a mermaid-head with knotted and dripping tresses, just from the swimming-pool, to beg Sydney's company and her violin below on the second floor. The invitation declined, the two were silent awhile.

II

Sydney, on the grey furry rug, trailed her slim length closer to the fire like a pale-green enchanted caterpillar.

"Did you hear Hilda on Marius at dinner?" she inquired drowsily. "She said if he hadn't stopped to bury his dead——"

"She's quite right. He is very beautiful but all wrong, you know. The supreme end of living——"

"Is fullness of life,"[31] cut in Sydney. "That's an axiom, like the being of a feeling is its being felt,[32] and that other, about the *esse* of a thing's being *percipi*.[33] Anyway, he had it, fullness of life. But it lands you in the Uebermensch,[34] all the same, and *he* is a fearful brute."

---

[31] This is a central tenet of Marius's philosophy, New Cyrenaicism (see *Marius the Epicurean*, Volume 1, Chapter IX).

[32] This seems to be an expression of the pragmatic philosophy of Charles Sanders Peirce (1839-1914).

[33] A principle in the philosophy of subjective idealism as espoused by George Berkeley in the 18th century. Berkeley expressed this in the combined Latin and English phrase, "*Esse* is *percipi*," that is, "To be is to be perceived."

[34] The *Übermensch* ("Over-Man," "Super-Man") is a concept in the philosophy of Friedrich Nietzsche, appearing most notably in his aphoristic work published as *Also Sprach Zarathustra* (German, 1885-1892), first translated into English, by Alexander Tille, as *Thus Spake Zarathustra* and published in 1896.

Mechanically Esther murmured: "Nonsense, the Uebermensch is the Magnanimous Man,[35] essentially."

"He's not a bit. Anyway, I don't believe you can work equations like that," replied Sydney, stretching up one hand pink against the fire. "I don't think the Magnanimous Man is the opposite of Marius and I know he isn't the same as the Uebermensch, even temperamentally. He risked greatly for great ends: Marius of course never risked at all but the Uebermensch is always chancing it for no particular reason. He doesn't go in for final causes,[36] does he? Please, between them I prefer the Aristotelian,—but not to know personally. It's bound to end in hardness."

"In the last analysis, your soul's your own," declared Esther with a habitual gesture of wrapping her gown about her, but the other broke in with a little cry:

"Ah, but it isn't! It's every one's else, in the last analysis."

"But it is not really so good in the long run even for the other people, that *Tristem Neminem Fecit*.[37] Remember Jane Barry, what she gave up for her people; they hadn't a thing against the man, but they couldn't spare her. Now they have an invalid, and when I was there at Christmas I noticed a very real hardness, which wasn't in the least pretty."

Sydney answered with a candour almost noble: "Really, of course, one should only make great renouncements on one's deathbed."

"Do you suppose that if Marlowe came by to-morrow and said: 'Chuck the degree, chuck Sydney there on the hearthrug, and come for a walk around the world,' I shouldn't go?"

"I suppose you would go, 'still climbing after knowledge infinite.'[38] But then you've no ties," finished Sydney, strong in the recollection of a father, a mother and several brothers and sisters.

---

[35] Variously translated as the Magnanimous Man, the proud man, or (perhaps most satisfactorily) the great-souled man or person, this is the ideal described by Aristotle in his *Nichomachean Ethics*, Book IV, Chapter 3.

[36] In Aristotle's scheme of the four causes for phenomena, the "final cause" is the purpose or goal of a phenomenon. See his *Metaphysics*, Book V, Chapter 2.

[37] The motto of Marius the Epicurean: "He made no one unhappy."

[38] A line from Christopher Marlowe's 1590 play, *Tamburlaine the Great*, Part I, Act II, Scene VII. Tamburlaine explains why he overthrows Cosroe, rather than helping the latter gain the Persian throne as Tamburlaine had promised:

"Don't you call yourself a tie?" laughed Esther.

"I believe you would go," Sydney repeated with a note of regretful admiration. "Now I pray I should have grace to reply: 'Thank you kindly, sir, but I'm bespoke.' I mean, if you had broken your back, for instance, or gone blind."

In an old oval mirror on the opposite wall Esther Lawes regarded for an instant her own fair strength, and the large grey eyes a little too clear and bright and round; from year to year they used to give out.

"I believe you would," she echoed, gazing down with her usual pleased sense of Sydney's beauty. Never did girl better match than Sydney Lodge her gracious name, radiant, the very sound of it, with sylvan and romantic suggestions. Her slimness had the graceless grace of Shakespeare's disguised heroines; her curls, of hair the most golden red, prompted the quaint Elizabethan epithet of "gold wires"; and her academic gown sat as straightly on her as the Oread's coat of sycamore bark.[39]

"God forbid," said Sydney Lodge solemnly. "The Powers have a trick now and then of taking us at our word, and our answered prayers are fruit bitter in the eating."

While she spoke they became conscious that the great bell was ringing, with strokes that sounded now near, now far distant, from every quarter, rhythmic in their pulse; the first distinct enough yet echoing familiarly, as though it were the second or third, the last in like manner seeming a faint intermediate one, whose successors the ear had lost. And like the wind awhile before, so the bell had a tang of darkness and the great spaces outside.

Nature, that fram'd us of four elements
Warring within our breasts for regiment,
Doth teach us all to have aspiring minds:
Our souls, whose faculties can comprehend
The wondrous architecture of the world,
And measure every wandering planet's course,
Still climbing after knowledge infinite,
And always moving as the restless spheres,
Will us to wear ourselves, and never rest,
Until we reach the ripest fruit of all,
That perfect bliss and sole felicity,
The sweet fruition of an earthly crown.

[39] An Oread is a type of nymph living in valleys, ravines, and mountains, according to Greek mythology.

III

In the house there were movements, and voices cut short by banging doors. Sydney had picked up a lamp and disappeared into her bedroom in a sphere of radiance, like a glow-worm. The dimmed room, which seemed yellower, took a new look: the whole Italian Renaissance, very adequately represented by the pictures on the walls, withdrew into itself and darkness. Esther stared absently from the long steamer chair at the faintly yellowed walls, at the pink bed of coals, and two Tanagra figurines above,—the lady who binds up her hair and the other lady carrying a wide basin in her slender hands, who forever bends over it to watch her own reflected face.

The girl was disturbed more by this fellowship business than even to her close friend she could betray. Not wanting the fellowship for herself, she did crave it for Sydney. Moreover, they could then go abroad together. She had longed that day to hint as much to a professor that was, she thought, disposed to overvalue her own rather advanced work along a very narrow line as against Sydney's all-round brilliancy. And while she heard the other opening drawers and rustling in her wardrobe, Esther pursued her misgiving a step further than it had ever before taken her, although at no time was she a fancier of illusions.

Their alliance, hers and Sydney's, ran back at least a dozen years, away into childhood, and was rooted in all sorts of mutual dependencies. Both moreover were fastidious and constant in their personal affections, making indeed few acquaintances but giving up fewer, and although Sydney had besides what the other called the goose-brigade, a succession of waddling and hissing creatures of both sexes that passed for swans, yet these never got farther than, so to speak, the common outside her windows. Esther herself, without near relatives and secure of a tiny income on which one could starve at least comfortably, having come to college in the interest less of culture than of pedantry, had in the interest of amusement supplemented her Greek with English, and her Hebrew, by way of serious study, with Assyrian and kindred tongues. But Sydney, positively, had gone through as many stages and as well-defined as a silk-worm. Once her violin was the be-all and the end-all; her masters had advised a professional training, urged the expediency of having a career up one's sleeve. Esther felt that it was she who had unconsciously lopped off that possibility,

in her own enthusiasm for the college which she was then about to
enter, to which she whirled off her friend, plumping her down mentally breathless in a field of Latin and Greek. For the past year or two
years, however, the classical prepossessions had been yielding to a
keener preoccupation with English and a kindling ambition along the
line of what the Sunday papers call literary work. This was furthered
partly by Esther's own growing delight in the same matters and partly
by the influence of other members of their class, notably Hilda Railton.

It was in the *argot* of their own vanishing here and now, of course,
that they had been talking, using counters precisely as the poker-
player does, to stand for an immense amount, or at any rate for an
indefinite amount. Sydney was wonderful at catching not merely the
turn of a phrase, but a turn of thought: she was *simpatica.*

"Do you know," said the voice from the inner room, "I can't get
that Japanese thing of Hilda's out of my head. Don't you think I might
look for one at that same Fifth Avenue place when I am at home at
Easter, and try it over my table?"

Hilda's Japanese print! There you were. After all, one did recog-
nize the type; it wasn't the superficial nor yet the parasite, but there
was about it something of the chameleon nature. It was the ominous
unruffled pool that brought Narcissus to his death. With all her brilliancy, all her charm, she was in essence simply the magical mirror.

Esther was convinced that neither Sydney herself knew this, nor
any of her neighbours. She was far and away too clever. There was just
one pathetic chance that somebody in the Faculty might be of so in-
conceivable a cleverness as to have spied the unscholastic fact.

For the third time that evening steps came to the door, and a
knock. Esther waited for Sydney and the girls moved together to the
threshold, opening on the mistress who held out an envelope. She
offered it to Esther.

IV

Is there any place in the world, Esther Lawes often in graduate
days asked her friends, where the evening light lies so long and so delicate as at Bryn Mawr? The campus, snow-piled, prolongs a pale dusk
at tea-time; in spring the afternoons grow longer slowly until they are
forgotten in the softness of the lengthening evenings; the great cherry-

tree, black against grey Pembroke but afoam and aflutter with exquisite whiteness, merges its sharp perfume into the softer odour of the
crowded flushed apple-trees and the pungent flavour of their neighbours the green-tufted larches. The misty woods back of Merion become denser aloft and under foot; and beyond the Roberts Road the
meadow fills up across the brook with pale shapely violets striped at
the heart by threads of purple; the long avenue of maples shakes out
its heavy leafage under which all day the girls with their rugs and cushions make yellow and scarlet splashes. After dinner, on the dense
short turf in front of Denbigh, she would watch the undergraduates
quadrilling—comely figures in faint blues and lavenders, ribbons and
ruffles all afloat. She stopped awhile on one of these bland nights in a
late and sudden spring, to scan the half-familiar types, the sleek heads
and white arms, in the waxing twilight, smiling to herself at her content
with them and with the swirl of voiceless swallows about one of the
high stone chimneys of Taylor Hall. Gathering up her own filmy dress
she moved through the deep-green grass that began to dull and chill
her slippers, to the shadowed postern door in the graduate wing and
up to her own study. She had not dreamed of such content, she remembered, her first night in the room.

V

All the days on the steamer she had misdoubted the return to
college after two years' absence, and the surprise and foreboding that
sprang up when her closest gaze at the dock failed to show her Sydney
Lodge, increased the mistrust. There was nothing for which to stay
over in New York since Sydney, according to the friends who did
show up to greet her, was still twenty miles off at the seashore, and
since Esther had cabled to engage the graduate suite of rooms for
themselves at college there was a place prepared and probably a letter
awaiting her there. Tired with the bustle of the custom house, she
scarcely noticed the sunburnt country north of Philadelphia, but from
the moment of pulling out from the city westward, found vague forgotten recollections stirring like indistinguishable odours.

Strong enough at last even to satisfy her was the sense of a glad
home-coming and the sudden contraction of her throat at particular
perceptions: the first glimpses of the bell-tower above the trees, the

stillness of the wind-swept air, the fresh and quiet beauty of the grey buildings and green turf.

As a simple mood she welcomed the feeling, prompt of course to pass, but equally prompt to return and supplant in time inevitable regrets for the other life now finally renounced.

It looked very gay, soft, desirable, that other life, while she surveyed the ungarnished and spotless emptiness of the bare study. On one table lay a pile of letters, the topmost directed in Sydney's hand so oddly like her own: a letter puzzling for the first sheet, then plain enough in its shamefaced announcement that the writer was engaged to be married—had been, indeed, for a month past but for some inexplicable reason had not wished Esther to learn before sailing. "H'm," thought Esther, "pity I didn't know this!" She looked around at the two study-tables, two lamps and two armchairs, almost the whole furniture of the room, and began to laugh. The stupid chair butting its nose against the table as maids always will leave study chairs, taunted her with the unnecessary assurance that Sydney would never occupy it.

The man in question, curiously enough, Esther had once known rather well. Her brother had been in the same class at Harvard, since whose death some years before she had scarcely seen him. But she had not heard of his meeting Sydney. He was a politician by trade, a lawyer by profession. He belonged in the Middle West.

Esther felt rather sick and very angry; Sydney at least needn't have made a fool of her! Still, she *could* see the comedy.

"Hello!" rang up a fine, strong voice below, and turning in the window-seat she saw on the grass brown sturdy Hilda Railton springing off her bicycle, rather warm and very pleased to see her. "I'm coming up. My room is down the hall. Let's have some tea!"

When the kettle had boiled Hilda remarked, as she shovelled in the tea: "So you're going in for the Ph. D. after all? I had dreamed you were strong-minded enough to resist the prevailing superstition. O Ichabod, Ichabod!"

Esther, laughing, echoed the *Ichabod* so sincerely that Hilda was prompted to change her ground and while she cut cool odorous slices of lemon to ask:

"So Sydney came back after one winter? I knew she would."

Esther answered rather dryly: "Yes, her family couldn't spare her."

"Sydney's family!" laughed Hilda, recognizing the object of hostility. "We all know it. 'Twas a pretty good year, wasn't it?"

"Ah, a golden year!"

"I had a notion from your letters last spring you were staying over there indefinitely. Then wasn't there a plan about Sydney's going back?"

"Yes. I needed more time. Last year my eyes played me a horrid trick and I couldn't work at all. Not even write letters," said Esther grimly. She had fancied it was because of her inability to answer that Sydney had written so seldom. "I had in another way almost as good a year idling about Berlin and Paris. My dear girl, you've no notion of the possibilities of idleness! So I quite thought of staying at the British Museum this winter, even alone, and finishing what I was at."

"Assyrian cylinders still?"[40]

"Always cylinders." This with a sudden sense of coldness. "The Deluge, and others. But I changed my mind." Never should any one, her former roommate least of all, know what had changed her mind. Actually this was a letter from Sydney Lodge, written in July and saying in effect, "I need you rather badly. How soon are you coming?" She had explained on a post-card that certain bricks and cylinders ought first to be deciphered and in the meantime had cabled for the rooms. She knew—it was one of the discoveries of this extraordinary afternoon—she knew Sydney's ways even to the point of prediction; that if she should say: "But my dear child I wrote you I had engaged the suite for us both," the young lady would answer with a brilliant smile of privilege and a new note—was it the sentimental?—in her voice: "Did you really? Well, I must have been thinking of something else when I read the letter." It was impossible not to laugh, but Esther covered the laughter with a sudden inspiration:

"Oh, I say, don't you want to share my study?"

"But Sydney?" cried poor Hilda, setting down her flowered teacup.

"Sydney's engaged. One Lewis Mason."

"Oh, dear!" Hilda answered flatly. "I'm rather sorry. I always believed in her, you know. She might have done things."

---

[40] Ancient Babylonians and Assyrians used a small cylinder with carved writing and scenes, as a sort of rolling seal. A collection of these has been held by the British Museum since the 19th century.

"Presumably one can do things with a husband. He is supposed to help," replied Esther, throwing forward her general convictions in the grotesque struggle for loyalty.

"Ah, she can't. And," added the girl, conclusively, "he won't."

"How's that?"

Hilda returned violently: "I know the beggar. She stayed a Sunday with Helen when I was there this summer and—he called in the evening. He's in politics, but quite respectable. I don't know why I shouldn't come, if you really want me: I'm taking my Ph. D., too, you know. Think it over. He's what they called," said Hilda with an explicit vagueness, "'*le parfait gentleman.*'"

VI

Esther looked around, when she went back to the emptiness, almost with a little shiver. This was the end then: *après tant de jours: après tant de fleurs.*[41] She had just for a little while known the unacademic world, people who had seen something different in her face, something rather sweet and rather sensitive.

How far all the things seemed and all alike how dim: the socialist meetings in Berlin, the cheap dinners at a droll *crêmerie* in Paris frescoed all around with the history of the Queen of Hearts and the immemorial tarts; even the soft after-dinner hour when she was staying with her cousins down in Leicestershire; even a delicious painter-boy who had just got into the Salon—all alike out of reach. The life before her looked poor and thin: books to be sure were at hand and one could hurry up to New York two or three times in a winter for the opera, and go abroad every summer with a companion chosen, like Hilda, expressly for her impersonality, one year to Greece, another time for the French cathedrals and *châteaux.*

---

[41] French: "After so many days: after so many flowers." One is tempted to think that *fleurs* here is a typographical error. The English Decadent poet Algernon Charles Swinburne had a line in a song within Act Four of his verse drama *Mary Stuart* (1881) to which Esther may be alluding here: *Après tant de jours: après tant de pleurs* ("After so many days: after so many tears").

Hilda—"she's impersonal as a Velasquez," she had written in the first week—proved for the aggrieved young woman the Griselda of companions.[42]

Even to herself Esther would only admit a few grounds of grievance. Sydney did well to marry, though there were elements of pain in the shock and the strangeness of her elected husband, but she, or somebody else, might have sounded a note of warning. That faint sigh of amorous trouble and the consequent precipitate response! Esther found herself in the position of one running at full speed who stops short, consciously red-faced and rather blown. The picture made her angry and undigested anger made her sick and spoiled her work.

There was even a sense of participation in Sydney's guilt, a secret confession of some dawdling in Paris, some philandering, that provoked to wholesome laughter. She had moments of saying to her inward interlocutor that it was rather absurd to chafe at the loss after all of only a few months, in June she would go back to London, to Paris, to the great glad world. But these conversations shared more or less the chimerical character of the thoughts when one lies awake at night and in the bodily warmth and darkness and the inner blaze of the overheated brain, one's perceptions, one's values are all monstrous. At last she saw that she had in truth been only playing with the thought of the straight, brown-bearded young artist in his little round cap like a Holbein drawing. Him she had not left behind without annoyance, though certainly she would not have wished to bring him along; but she could not even for Sydney have left behind her lexicons and manuscripts, and comical little bricks done up in pasteboard jewel boxes.

VII

The moon plainly was coming up in a hurry behind Dalton as Esther paused at the entrance to her room, for though still invisible it filled with light the air outside all the windows. Against this pale-blue background Hilda on the sill was making coffee in a tall green porcelain pot. The air was full of the spicy steam.

---

[42] The folktale character Griselda was legendary for her extreme obedience and long-suffering.

"*Dégenérée!*" laughed Esther. "Didn't you have coffee for dinner?"

"Dinner was a long time ago," replied Hilda sententiously. "Besides, I didn't have enough. Where have you been? Your frock is clammy."

"In the Harriton family graveyard, first, sitting on the steps over the wall and listening to a woodthrush. Did you ever have enough?" Esther added, lighting a lamp as she spoke, while the brass teakettle winked in the soft light and the outside earth vanished. "Hilda, it's a good world."

"A well-enough world," answered Hilda crossing the yellow patch to get the delicate cups. As she returned with them Esther studied her black serge skirt and caught it up.

"Cat-hairs!" she affirmed. "How was Helen?—I've not seen her for a long time. And how was Pasht? He has a black soul."

"He's uncommonly beautiful. If you go to Chapel to-morrow," said Hilda irrelevantly, "you will hear the President announce that I am appointed a Reader in English for next year. Pretty good, isn't it, for a Canadian who is Scotch?"

"That's all right, Doctor Railton," murmured Esther congratulating her and adding, "Then I'm sure of you here next year." This was before the days of Low Buildings, and Readers lived in the Halls where and how they could.

Esther lay back in her chair, admiring the tarnished frame of a quaint oval mirror that reflected a really admirable Japanese watercolour of Hilda's. She was glad the study would be unchanged another year, and quiet. She thought, too, with a little shudder of the hot bad air of crowded rooms, the loud noise of voices, the indecorous bustle of a life made up of many acquaintances.

"I am going to Spain this summer to look at some Arabic manuscripts," she said at length. "You'd better come too. If we cross cheaply and don't travel we can live on nothing. Berenson says the Spanish galleries are full of wonderful pictures, practically unknown."

"My dear, I've a family," laughed Hilda ruefully.

"Didn't you say last night that they were going to the winds of heaven this year and that you didn't know what to do? Represent to them, moreover, that one shouldn't lose so superb a chance of *doing* me. Seriously, I shall take a whole stateroom, not having forgotten the seasick German girl I came home with last time, and you'd much better occupy the other berth. Indeed, I can't travel alone in Spain, you know."

Her eyes were fixed on eighteen square inches of pinkish brocade pinned against the wall—her Christmas present to Hilda and a ruinous extravagance. A chance word, from a lecture, she had caught up and fancied once, came back: "Nobody frames the multiplication table and hangs it on the wall." But surely that was because the multiplication table was shallow and petty and strikingly untrue: there were tracts of knowledge infinite and unfathomable where one would never tire.

The things, she realized, which one does not ask too much of—and the people—are the things which are forever surprising one with unguessed possibilities.

"Curiosity, after all, is the only insatiable emotion," said Esther out of her experience, and there were always more little bricks: one might even in time when one had read all the rest, go and dig some up with one's own hands.

Georgiana Goddard King, '96.

STUDIES IN COLLEGE COLOUR

The great bell clangs out through the morning air—through the snowflakes that thicken it, sending its summons over the white-crusted campus. The slippery walks are crowded with black figures moving towards Taylor Hall, single, in groups of twos and threes, wrapped close with shawls and hoods, half of them umbrellaless. Voices fall as they enter and amid friendly jostling around the bulletin board and in the cloak-room whispered greetings are exchanged. Then upstairs to the silent chapel, with its white windows made whiter by the frost; a stillness seeming to fold it round. The black mortar-boards nod their tassels in cheery greeting; subdued talk between neighbours fills the room with a low hum. A sudden hush; the talk stops; the heads are still; a moment's pause and the service has begun. All are together for once in the day, with no distinctions of class or grade. All are alike children, and children of Bryn Mawr. At the close of the prayer another moment's silence. Then a sudden movement. The bell clangs out again. A general rush to classes, to the office, to one's room. The day has begun.

❖   ❖   ❖

The sunlight is streaming in through the broad windows. It dances among the leaves of the red geraniums on the window-sill and falls upon the carpet in bright spots and bands. The bookcase and the two shelves of the little mahogany desk are crowded with a confusion of much worn, many-coloured volumes. Over the Dresden inkstand and disordered files of papers and pencils a small brass dragon mounts guard. Dainty cups shine on the white tea-table, which bears for its motto the words of the March Hare:

> *"It's always tea-time, and we've no time to wash the tea things between whiles."*

On the Turkish scarf which drapes the mantel stands a ginger-jar full of yellow roses. Across the rocking-chair is thrown a college gown, while tennis balls and rackets strew the floor. The divan is filled with flowered cushions innumerable, and half-buried among them is the mistress of all this colour and confusion. She is reading "The Republic."

It was a warm afternoon in May. The shadows were lengthening on the campus, and the air had all the stillness of midsummer. On the grass near the gravel walk a robin was hopping and pecking. Two black-gowned figures had just passed slowly by, and now all was still again. A sparrow who had been hovering for several minutes over head alighted close by the robin.

"Ah!" said the robin, "could you but fancy what you have lost! Two seniors conversing together. Did you not perceive them?"

The sparrow would gladly have concealed his ignorance on such classic ground, yet, constrained by curiosity, with hanging head he asked, "What may seniors be?"

"Seniors," replied the robin. "Do you not know, then, that seniors are the sovereigns of this place? Indeed, I assure you, it is true. We have their own confession for it. Listen while I tell you the words of these two as they passed by.

"'Well, it is almost over,' said one. 'And next year what do you suppose will become of the college?'

"'It is too dreadful to think of,' said the other. 'Some of our class may come back as graduates. That is the only hope.'

"'And even then they cannot help the Undergraduate Association. And they will be too few to manage Self-Government. Oh, this dear old college! It is too terrible to think of leaving it to go to rack and ruin. And just when everything is in the best condition possible! Imagine the Editorial Board without some member from '93! And the standard of class work is sure to fall next year.'

"'And the gymnasium, too. To be sure most of us are making up conditions in the gym, but then——'

"'Oh, there is no help for it! The college is sure to go down now. And it has been rapidly rising for four years! It is too cruel!'"

The robin paused. Then he hopped confidingly towards the sparrow and, cocking his head on one side, whispered, "If you will take the trouble to listen you will hear conversations like that every spring on this campus. Now you know what seniors are."

L. S. B. S., '93; G. E. T. S., '93.

EPOCH MAKING

The morning after the freshman play found the gymnasium looking somewhat forlorn. The portable stage had lost part of the discreet drapery that masked its front below the footlights, and now recklessly displayed its crazy supports to the public eye; the footlights themselves were a mass of blackened tallow in their battered tin sockets; the faded green canton-flannel curtains which had served as a forest background for the last act of *Prince Otto*,[43] and been torn from half their rings at its end when Seraphina and the prince tried to make a simultaneous entry in response to applause, trailed limply from their remaining supports, and seemed to beg for the friendly shadows of the property-room to hide their rents and tatters. In the corners of the stage, the groups of branches which had simulated the primeval forest drooped their withered heads in mournful wise against their too evident props, and like the grey cambric rocks and tin-foil rivulet which occupied the centre of the scene, were hardly recognizable as parts of last night's fairy woodland.

Even less recognizable, but scarcely so forlorn, the actors in the performance soon began to drop in, at first one by one, and then in little groups of two or three. They came in fresh and smiling and full of misdirected zeal for the work of clearing up; most of the later arrivals came from the basket-ball field, and flung down their gaily-coloured golf-capes just where they would be most in the way; and all of them, as they went about pulling down the decorations, and piling borrowed properties into bewildering heaps for return to their owners, chattered incessantly of last night's great success.

The November sunlight fell in yellow, dusty shafts through the high windows above the running track, spilling its pale brightness on the cluttered floor and stage, and spread even into the alcove where the horizontal bars jostled the horse and the rowing-machines in ignominious confusion and with a general shamefaced air of being huddled out of the way. The position of the yellow rays indicated ten o'clock, and the busy workers, having accumulated rugs, curtains, cos-

---

43 The freshman play must have been a stage adaptation of the novel of the same title by Robert Louis Stevenson, first published in 1885.

tumes, bric-a-brac, a number of potted plants, and the fragments of a pasteboard fireplace, in heterogeneous piles on every side, were beginning to wonder if they could ever straighten them out again, when the arrival of three or four fresh recruits gave them an excuse for resting while they reported progress.

Their labours, indeed, spoke for themselves. Peggy Dillon, the class chairman, who headed the reinforcements, opened her round blue eyes aghast at the dusty chaos which greeted her, and found herself bereft of speech by the look of modest pride which beamed from all the faces before her; but one of her companions, a handsome girl with a certain air of authority about her, was equal to the occasion.

"Dear me, how enterprising you all are!" she exclaimed, coming forward with a comprehensive smile; "there is really a great deal accomplished already. (Don't look so utterly overcome, Peggy, if you can help it.) You must have worked like beavers to get all those curtains down."

The workers, hot, dirty, and dishevelled, beamed with redoubled brightness upon the speaker, and upon the havoc they had wrought, and tasted all the sweetness of being appreciated. Pauline Van Sandford was a tall girl who carried her head rather high, and spoke with a good-humoured imperiousness. Perhaps these things added weight to her remarks. With a very creditable show of gratification, she went on,

"And nearly all the properties in piles!" Here a gasp from Peggy, who had just discovered her pet cast in one of the said piles under a section of the stage-steps, warned her to hasten her climax; she worked up her remarks to quite an enthusiastic close, and then, apparently consumed with anxiety for the workers' fatigue, she fell upon the helpful band, and fairly swept them from the gymnasium upon a wave of appreciative solicitude.

"Do go home and lie down, all of you—no, it's really too much to expect—no, don't think of staying, we can do all the rest—no, you are too good, and we are awfully grateful, but—there!" She slammed the door upon the bewildered objects of her gratitude, and then, falling back against it, exchanged looks of despair with her companions.

"Who would ever have thought they'd get at it so early!" wailed Peggy, on her knees beside a particularly hopeless-looking heap of articles; "will some one help me to rescue my poor Clytie? Shirley, lend a hand with these steps."

Shirley Nairn, a slender girl with a big, soft, dust-brown pompa-dour, brown eyes, and a firm little chin which half contradicted their gentleness, began cautiously to lift away the boards. She had a flutter-ing grace in all her movements like that of a bird just lighting. "Rescue is the word," she said; "there is still hope for most of the things, but unless we do a lot before lunch, those Vandals will be back again, and next time there will be nothing left but chips."

In spite of the discouraging outlook, an hour or two of hard work did wonders. Curtains and costumes went to the property-room, the faded forest hid its head in a corner, the borrowed chairs and rugs and rubber-plants found themselves grouped in something like order, and the rescue party sank at last upon a mattress in the alcove to wipe its heated brow, and survey results.

"There is less damage done than you would think," observed Katharine Holland; she was a girl of that ineffectual type that must al-ways appeal to some one, and she now turned her long brown face and mournful eyes towards Shirley. "Except for Peggy's Clytie, and a few smashed pots, and that long tear in Miss Meredith's leopard-skin, most things seem to have been miraculously spared. There is a special Providence that watches over idiots."

Still inspecting her very grimy hands, Shirley said, "They aren't really idiots, but you can't leave them to themselves. We should have had a committee."

"It's all my fault; I neglected it," began Peggy meekly.

"We are all just as bad," Pauline interrupted in a decided tone; "Louise is stage manager, and I am business manager, and look at our behaviour: we have both been wasting valuable time on our essay ap-pointments when we should have been attending to business."

As self-accusation seemed the order of the day, each of the small party came forward to blame herself, and did it thoroughly and at some length. When a soothing pause came at last, Shirley said medita-tively,

"I heard Miss Meredith say the other day that women couldn't work together effectively, because woman isn't a political animal."

Charlotte Meredith's masters degree and undisputed cleverness gave no small weight to her opinion among the undergraduates, but Pauline, as her cousin and protégée, stood less in awe of her than most of the freshmen; she had even dared to christen her, quite open-ly, "the Cynic." It was Pauline, therefore, who now voiced the meeting's dissent from Miss Meredith's dictum. Woman could be a political animal, if she chose, and was properly directed. All that the class of '9_ needed was to be taught to think before they acted.

Louise Ferguson, a small bustling girl with red hair, wanted to know how you were going to teach them to think. They might be able to do it separately, but when you took them in the mass, they were just like a flock of sheep, and class meetings merely a game of follow-my-leader. No matter how clever and sensible the individual girl was, a class of sixty-three girls was capable of any idiocy on the spur of the moment. "Look at the number of classes who elect their presidents, and then hate them ever after. Look at the case of the class who barred out their temporary chairman, and then spent the rest of their college career wishing they had elected her. They never know what they want, or if they do, they don't know enough to get it."

"Thanks awfully," crowed Peggy; "all the bouquets are coming my way. '9_ made me chairman, therefore they did not want me. Q.E.D. Thanks ever so much!"

As Louise and Peggy were roommates, their differences could be left for private settlement. Louise therefore took no notice of this interruption, beyond a threatening scowl at the speaker, and, sticking bravely to her point, appealed to Pauline for support. In Pauline's opinion class politics were usually unintelligent, but she did not agree that there was no help for it. When the spirited discussion which this remark brought on had run its rather ineffectual course to no conclusion, the two disputants fell silent, and four of the little group found themselves looking shyly at Shirley Nairn.

Three of the girls had come up together from the Airlie School in New York, and Pauline Van Sandford was their leader; Peggy Dillon was a Philadelphia girl who had chanced upon a room in the "Airlie corridor" of Pembroke East, and whose short-lived ascendency in '9_'s affairs had declined, very early in her chairmanship, into dependence upon Pauline; but Shirley Nairn lived in Merion, and the four knew very little about her, except that her schoolmates from the Briony School of New Haven counted on her to win the class presidency from the Airlie candidate. So now they eyed her sideways, and waited for her views on class politics as expressing class intelligence; and the pause was just beginning to be uncomfortable when she lifted her head.

"We might try to better things in our own case," she said tentatively; "there ought to be a way to make class politics intelligent, but we can only prove it by doing it."

"How?" asked Louise, while Pauline rapidly decided that Shirley Nairn did not have that square chin for nothing. Then, taking the floor herself, Pauline opined that the whole trouble lay in too hasty action. "We women," she said, rather grandly, and with her usual air of decided conviction, "we women make up our minds before we think; we look at a few arguments, listen to our friends' opinions, leap to a conclusion (usually all wrong), and score another foolish vote."

Peggy's groan of mock despair, which followed this speech, and was meant to preface a lively protest, was robbed of effect by the sudden sound of Taylor bell, ringing for lunch-time; and the parliament of five forthwith dissolved. But as they dispersed, Pauline pledged them all to come to her room that evening for further discussion of the subject. They met there accordingly, with a few other high souls who were ripe for reform; they discussed; and from their discussion there grew a plan.

When the class of '9_ assembled a few days later in Denbigh Students' Parlour, they expected to nominate and forthwith elect their permanent officers; but on the latter point a considerable surprise was in store for them. After the nomination votes for president were cast and counted, and the result announced—Shirley and Pauline far in the lead, and very close together, Peggy a modest third, and a few other names straggling hopelessly in the rear—the chairman rose to tell them that a change in the usual order of proceedings was proposed. The nominations for president were now before them; the election was postponed, by order of the chair, until that day week, in order that during the interval the class might weigh well its measures before taking the final—Peggy's tone almost implied, the fatal—step. In the stupefied silence which followed this announcement, she went on to give the arguments in favour of the new course. It would give them time to look into the qualifications of the candidates and form their decision intelligently; it would prevent mistakes which they might deplore hereafter; and—superbly—it would mark the beginning of a new epoch in class politics. The candidates were bound in honour not to canvass for themselves, or to allow others to do so, and the final ballot was to be cast according to each voter's conviction of what would be best for the class. No haste in deciding, no prejudice, no regard to personal influ-

ence; but careful consideration, and final action on the highest and
most disinterested grounds—that was the idea.

When the other nominations were in, and the meeting ad-
journed, the class of '9_ went its various ways homeward sorely bewildered. It does not do, as a rule, to call upon a freshman class for too
much disinterested consideration when it is just recovering from the
effects of a freshman play; but the undergraduate mind will usually
rise to a hook that is baited with the word "epoch-making." So the
members of '9_ eager to make an epoch, fell very earnestly and ardently to work at the business of weighing and comparing the two
chief candidates before them; Peggy's name was very little under discussion, for her chances were hardly to be considered seriously, and,
as interest centred in the presidency, the candidates for other offices
got very little attention. But concerning the merits and demerits of
Shirley and Pauline, the course of debate ran high and warm; during
the seven days assigned them, the freshmen talked of little else, and
strove hard to prove, by quite a heated exhibition of partisan spirit,
that they were political animals after all, while the two principal nomi-
nees affected an Olympian indifference to the result, and used a dignified reserve when greeting each other in the corridors of Taylor. And
amused upper classmen made laughing guesses as to the outcome of
the campaign.

But the new plan did not work exactly as its framers had expected, and in a day or two there were rumours that things were going
wrong. By the middle of the week these rumours had gathered such
strength that Charlotte Meredith, M. A., and Fellow of Bryn Mawr
College, felt called upon to visit her freshman cousin, and hear the
news. Accordingly she knocked at the door of 39 Pembroke East on
the afternoon of the fifth day following the nominations. Charlotte
Meredith, whom Pauline called the Cynic, was a tall, slight girl, pale
and clean-looking, with quantities of very black hair; she had bright,
near-sighted grey eyes behind her glasses, and walked with a stoop;
her usual expression was one of whimsical boredom. There was probably no one in the world whom Pauline would have cared less to see
at her door that afternoon, but she welcomed the unexpected guest
with almost her usual readiness, and tried to cover the real hollowness
of her greeting by eager hospitality in the line of tea and jam. Peggy
was there, too, spreading crackers with a worried air; and both girls
seemed somewhat harassed by Charlotte's questions as to the outlook

for the election, delivered with her habitual slight drawl and air of fa-
tigued politeness.

"I take a lively interest in it," she told them, in a tone expressive
of anything rather than liveliness, as she stirred her tea; "and I hope
you won't let the fact that you are both candidates embarrass you.
This impersonal campaign of yours is highly novel, and your effort to
elevate class politics into a thing of moral beauty smacks delightfully of
altruism, but may I ask how the thing is likely—in the vulgar phrase—to
pan out?" She nibbled her cracker appreciatively, and gave the dis-
comfited pair a questioning smile. Peggy squirmed a little, and said
nothing; but Pauline burst out,

"The whole affair is too miserable and humiliating for words, and
has panned out like—like—Charlotte, it is literally past speech! I am
ashamed of belonging to such a small-minded sex, for the girls have
acted abominably."

Charlotte smiled benignly. "As I understand that your reform is
in part a crusade against a statement of mine that woman is not a political animal, would you mind telling me whether their abominableness
throws any light on that point?"

"Political animals?" cried Pauline; "I should say they were! If we
have a rag of reputation left by the end of the week, I shall be surprised."

"And by 'we' you mean——"

"Shirley Nairn and myself; Peggy seems to have been spared."

"Yes," Peggy assented with the utmost affability, "they are after
bigger game, thank Heaven!" And then, the flood-gates being opened,
Charlotte was favoured with a full, if not very coherent account of
'9_'s enormities. Events had taken a course which was not to be wondered at. In the ranks of '9_, deliberation had brought on discussion,
discussion had led to dispute; and in the clash of warring factions,
each side had brought so many charges of unfitness against the oppos-
ing candidate that Pauline declared her own character, as well as
Shirley's, blackened for life.

"That is doing fairly well for a purely impersonal campaign not
yet five days old," was Charlotte's grim comment; "I suppose you do
not lack for friends to keep you posted on the state of public opinion."

"My dear Miss Meredith," responded Peggy genially, "the only
reason that the door is not at this moment besieged with news from

the seat of war is that the rest of the class are at freshman drill, which Pauline and I are sinfully cutting. Only think, Polly, how their tongues are wagging even now! And how——"

A resounding knock at the door cut her short.

"There!" she groaned resignedly, "drill must be over. Come in!" And as the three turned towards the door, Pauline said savagely, "Here come all my dearest friends!"

But it was Shirley Nairn who pushed the door open, and at sight of Charlotte stopped doubtfully on the threshold. Over her shoulder, they saw the frightened face of Katharine Holland. Shirley was looking at Pauline.

"I have something rather important to say," she said; "it concerns us both, and"—she hesitated for a barely appreciable second—"and no one else. Except Miss Holland," frigidly, with a glance over her shoulder.

"Oh, come in, come in!" cried Pauline, "and if it is about this wretched election, let us have it out. Charlotte and Peggy know the worst, I think. Come in."

Shirley advanced, and Katharine shrinkingly followed her; the uneasy air of the latter, and her apprehensive looks, made Charlotte sit up with an expression of interest.

"The plot thickens," she soliloquized to her teacup; and Pauline, hearing her, knit her brows impatiently.

"Well?" she said rather shortly to Shirley. Her tone brought a flush to the other's cheek; she hesitated for another moment, and then said coldly,

"Miss Holland will explain."

Upon being brought thus abruptly into prominence, Katharine Holland silently besought them all for mercy with her shamed eyes; then, urged by a monitory look from Shirley, who leaned beside the table in frozen silence, she brought out a foolish and pitiable tale. It was simply an account of various silly slanders, some directed against Shirley, and others against Pauline, with which she confessed she had regaled a company of upper classmen, apparently only to amuse them; and she interrupted her confession with weak excuses, like a guilty child. In her humiliation she made an uncomfortable spectacle, but Shirley said sternly, "Finish."

"Oh, let her be!" cried Pauline, impatient of the scene; "who cares to hear all this? We know it already."

"There is one thing yet," said Shirley, "but I will tell it myself; I made her tell all the rest, so that you might know whether you ought to take her word against me. She has accused me of going about to ask for votes." The speaker's tone was stout enough, but she leaned heavily on the table, "so I brought her here to retract it."

Stung by a generous indignation, Pauline sprang to her feet. "Would you have believed that of me?" she cried. "She need not trouble to retract it." Then, turning to Katharine, "That is quite enough, Miss Holland," she said, and the penitent stumbled to the door.

As the door closed upon her, Charlotte, who had finished her tea in silence, put down her cup with an air of decision, and turning to Shirley, said suddenly,

"Wasn't it a little hard on her, Miss Nairn?"

"To punish her for telling a campaign lie?" demanded Shirley.

"Please leave the campaign out of the question for a moment. She doesn't seem particularly venomous; don't you think she deserved a little mercy?"

"She is a poor creature," said Shirley setting her lips, "and deserves nothing."

"She is a poor creature," Charlotte assented in her easy drawl, "whom you have made poorer by the loss of her self-respect. Why?"

"Because she lied about us," retorted Pauline, rushing in to defend their joint position.

"Would you even have given her lies a thought," asked her cousin with a little more animation, "if they hadn't interfered with your precious campaign? You have just made her pay for your own mistake in attempting the impossible; you began by trying impersonality in politics, and you have ended by humiliating a classmate for indulging in a few exaggerated personalities at your expense. Is it very consistent?"

Struck dumb by surprise at this attack, Pauline did not answer, but Shirley broke in, with hot cheeks,

"It was a case of self-defence, Miss Meredith."

Charlotte, as she rose to go, smiled complete comprehension into the younger girl's troubled eyes; it was easy to see that the rivals already valued each other's good opinion beyond the votes of the class, and she scented fresh developments. "They won't be a bad team," she decided on her way home.

Her departure left the other three somewhat at a loss for words, but Shirley, with an evident effort, broke the uncomfortable silence.

"We've made a mistake somewhere," she said hopelessly, "and everything has gone miserably wrong; but I hope you will believe that I meant well, even in bringing Katharine Holland here." And she turned towards the door.

"Don't go," said Pauline; "sit down, and have some tea." Then seeing that the other hesitated, "You know that I don't care a rap about those tales, and I know that you don't either," she said, stoutly. "I am glad that you came. Won't you please stay?"

Peggy, who had been absorbed in circumventing the treacherous tendencies of her jam-sandwich, emerged victorious from the struggle to say soothingly,

"Nobody ever believes campaign lies, anyway."

"Except the voters," was Shirley's dry response, as she dropped into a chair.

During the next half-hour, both Pauline and Shirley announced their unalterable intention of withdrawing from the race; each declared that, for the good of the class, the other ought to be president, but neither would consent to her rival's retiring, so that, as Peggy said, the only way out was for both to stay in. The debate ended in a decision to abide the issue, and ignore the slanderous tongues, whereupon they parted much uplifted in spirit, and were very solemn at dinner that night, as befitted noble-hearted victims who suffered for their efforts to elevate their kind.

On the evening before the election, Charlotte Meredith caught Shirley in the act of waylaying an Airlie freshman in the hall. Her victim, in gymnasium dress, with her mask and foil, was evidently overdue at a fencing-lesson, and anxious to be off, but Shirley was pitiless, and pinned her to the spot, while she discoursed at length.

"The impersonal campaign is still on, I see," murmured Charlotte, as she passed.

Shirley's face blazed. "I was telling her the truth as to some lies about Pauline," she flashed out, and then looked as if she could have bitten her tongue for speaking.

The freshman, grateful for an interruption, escaped.

"You needn't have told me that you were canvassing for Pauline, any more than Pauline needed to tell me this morning, when I met her coming out of a Briony girl's room, that she was canvassing for you. A fine consistent pair you are! But it won't make any difference," she added, darkly, with a return to her usual whimsical manner.

The evening of the election buried the reform fathoms deep; for Peggy was elected president. When the little band of reformers entered the students' parlour, where the class was already assembled, they received the impression of a huddled flock of sheep, with lowered heads at bay. The evening's proceedings deepened this impression. The class of '9_ was worried and bewildered and disgusted; it had travailed in the throes of indecision until it sickened of both alternatives, and fell, like many another, upon the middle course. That course was the choice of Peggy, astonished Peggy, by an overwhelming majority in the good old follow-my-leader fashion; while Pauline and Shirley watched their airy fabric of reform topple to ruin, and then talked of other things during the counting of the votes.

Charlotte Meredith laughed over the result with the rest of the on-lookers, but, rather surprisingly, took the part of the would-be reformers, after a subtle fashion of her own. "After all," she remarked, with an air of elaborate deference to a loudly critical sophomore, "even you and I, Miss West, were freshmen once." And Miss West turned a slow red, and refrained from speech.

It was Charlotte's custom to have her freshman cousin at most of her small teas, so Pauline found nothing remarkable in the appearance, about this time, of a small card on her table, reading, "Tea at five. C. M."; but it was embarrassingly unusual to find in her cousin's study, not the expected circle of graduates, with a senior or two, but only Charlotte herself and Shirley Nairn. The two guests were duly regaled with tea and bonbons by Miss Meredith, who, ignoring late events, tried to put them at their ease. In her whimsical way, she liked them both. There was, however, a spark of covert amusement in her eyes as she passed the teacups; and Pauline, writhing inwardly under this satirical observation, finally came out with:

"I suppose you were pleased with the result of our campaign."

"Naturally," said Charlotte blandly. "One likes to have a guess confirmed—and I was sure of the result; in that way I was pleased. And you?"

Pauline, playing with her teacup, remarked that people weren't usually pleased with having made fools of themselves. Her tone asked for a contradiction, but it did not come, and the three sat silent, listen-

ing to the singing of the kettle over the spirit-flame, until Shirley said
abruptly:

"Miss Meredith, you were right about the political animals."

Charlotte raised her eyebrows enquiringly, but was perhaps not
surprised by what she heard; she may have already reflected that defeat, always hard to bear, comes in its most unbearable form when it
makes its victims ridiculous. Shirley and Pauline, having been baulked
by very small means in a project of mighty import, had a galling sense
of the absurdity of their position, and were bitterly ready to turn on
their ungrateful classmates. Therefore Charlotte had the satisfaction of
seeing them come over to her point of view with exaggerated enthusiasm. They could not put too strongly the impossibility of any attempt
to educate women politically; they thought that a few—a very few, they
sadly added—might be trusted for public-spirited and disinterested action; but the mass of women were not large-minded enough to rise
above personal considerations.

"What other considerations did the poor things have, in your
case?" asked their hostess. "A class president's duties are not so
weighty that she needs any distinguished qualifications, and the choice
is simply a matter of personal liking. You insisted on a week's analysis
of personal likes and dislikes, and the natural result was exaggeration
and slander."

The freshmen sat in crestfallen silence. They had acknowledged
their defeat; must they now acknowledge that it was deserved? Putting
down her plate and leaning a little forward in her chair, Charlotte regarded them earnestly.

"Let me tell you something," she said; "I have not lived in college
six years for nothing; I have learned a great deal in that time; but it did
not take me six years to learn not to waste my energy on trifles. In this
campaign of yours, you have used up an amount of force which would
have accomplished wonders in a serious cause. Has it paid?"

"I'm afraid not," they said.

"It is an odd thing, too," said Charlotte, in a casual tone, "to notice that in nine cases out of ten the popular instinct is a safer guide
than the popular reason. Your class reasoned itself into a frenzy, and
then, by instinct, did the right thing."

At this unexpected tribute to their conqueror, the two vanquished
leaders looked a bit blank; perhaps they had nursed a faint egotistical
hope of some day seeing the class brought to a realizing sense of its

mistake in electing Peggy, and Charlotte's view was a blow. She saw the effect of her words.

"They did the right thing," she repeated, "in choosing a girl who will be an excellent figurehead for—a coalition—" Charlotte smiled, a little self-complacently; she rather prided herself on the sensitiveness of her feeling for things that were in the air—"a public-spirited, disinterested——"

"Oh, don't!" pleaded Shirley; "I am sick of it. We have been talking awful cant, haven't we?"

"Suppose we talk about that," said Charlotte.

And they did. They talked about it until the late sunlight faded, and twilight came down on the little study; and then, in the gathering gloom, they talked about it still, and all the more freely. The older girl, who had tilted with windmills in her time, opened her heart to these young Quixotes, fresh from their first fall, on the difference between cant and college spirit; and the two freshmen, sitting in the twilight with tingling cheeks, pledged themselves silently to the larger vision.

As they wended their way homeward across the dusky campus, they were very silent; when Pauline spoke once, it was only to say, "I am sorry I called her the Cynic."

And Charlotte, watching their dark receding forms as she leaned from her open window, hoped that she hadn't been preaching. It was the old, old antithesis between enthusiasm and experience; and after all there was much to be said for enthusiasm. Those two youngsters had brought something out of their mischance, if it was only their liking for each other. "I wish I were a freshman again," sighed Charlotte to the stars.

Cora Armistead Hardy, '99.

A REMINISCENCE

We had met, after two years or so out in the "wide, wide world" of which we had sung so dolefully, the last weeks of senior year. I discovered that Evelyn had substituted soft "fluffs" for the stiff collars she had clung to tenaciously through four years of college, and she admitted that after the first shock she quite liked the new way I did my hair. Later she also admitted that she made a practice of carrying a parasol, or even of wearing a hat, when it was excessively sunny. Emboldened by the confession, I ventured to produce some embroidery and went to work as if such femininity had always been my pose. Then we talked, and exchanged various bits of news about the members of the class who had wandered so far since our separation.

"Wasn't it sad about Janet?" I asked at last. And then as Evelyn kept silent, I went on, "you knew, didn't you?—She died last November just a little while after her engagement was announced. It was typhoid fever. I thought you knew, of course."

"Yes, I knew," said Evelyn, and went on examining the bookcase.

"I think I'll tell you about it," she exclaimed at last. "It won't do any good. But I think I'd like to tell you. You know Janey and I were awfully good friends while she was at college. We even thought of rooming together, but we were both so well satisfied with our single suites that we decided not to. We were almost like roommates, though. Janet always saw that I was registered when I went home and I always stole rolls for her when she was locked out from breakfast. We wore each other's clothes indiscriminately. I have one of her handkerchiefs yet. You know how it was. We were just awfully good friends."

"I know—Janet would do anything under the sun for any one she liked—go on."

"Well, then she left college. She didn't like it—one bit. She was perfectly frank and said she wanted to come out before she was twenty. Do you know how it is in those western towns? They think a girl is antique when she's twenty-one. She came out and was a great success, I believe. You know how she stopped writing to first one, then another of us, and we were all rather hurt about it."

"Well, she *was* a disappointment. I had always thought her so superbly loyal, and we heard that she said college was 'such a bore.'"

"Yes, I believed that too, but not until I had written several letters after she had stopped. Finally I gave up and thought I'd never hear from her again. I felt pretty bitter about it. At last she wrote me and told me of her engagement. Just the real old Janey, it was—called me by some absurd nickname she'd invented, confessed that she'd been horrid about not writing, and then said that although the engagement wasn't to be announced immediately, she wanted me to be one of the first to know, and would I congratulate her?"

"When was this?" I asked, after a pause. Evelyn had seized my scissors and seemed to be too much interested in snipping ends of embroidery silk to remember Janet or me, or any one else. She dropped the scissors and took up a book of college kodaks. I repeated my question, just to remind her that I was still there.

She turned her back and went on. "That was some time in May. It came to me at a most unpropitious time. Some member of the family had been ill and I was tired and cross and feeling unjustifiably righteous. So I sat down then and there and told poor old happy Janet how nice and high-minded I had been about writing and how unfriendly she had been. I said of course I hoped she would be happy and all that but of course after this long hiatus we could never be friends in the same old way. Oh, it was an icy letter, just as politely nasty as I could make it! I sent it off and afterwards I felt just exactly the way I used to when I was a small child and had been naughty and wanted to make up. But I didn't. I tried to forget it. I was very busy and had a lot of people visiting me, last summer. So the thought of Janet didn't come into my head very often and when it did I mentally changed the subject. Of course I never heard from her again.

"One day, after we came back to town I was reading, not thinking of anything but the book—Janey least of all. Nothing in that book could have reminded me of her. I read it over afterwards to see. I looked up all of a sudden, thinking of Janet—thinking of her as if I had been with her an hour before. I dropped the book and felt as if I had just seen her, standing at the door in a familiar kimono, and heard her addressing me for the first time by that ridiculous nickname that she had just invented. I had heard through some people from her town that she was going to be married soon. My pride simply vanished. I dashed up and wrote her in the good old friendly way, told her what a

nice lady she was and how often I thought of her, what I had been doing, and all sorts of natural old things, as if I had been writing to her
regularly for years. I sent that letter off wondering if she would answer.
Two days later I heard somehow that she had typhoid fever, but I
thought that if she got my letter she would surely answer somehow,
though she had been ill for days then."

Evelyn turned and showed me a photograph of herself and Janet
laughing and entwined in an attitude of exaggerated affection.

"The next thing I heard of Janey," she continued, "was the news
of her death and I shall never know whether she received my letter."

Clara Warren Vail, '97.

CATHERINE'S CAREER

"Now, Jack, please don't be sentimental. You know how I hate it. Besides you have interrupted me just when I was convincing you that education will solve the race problem, and that is annoying." Poor Jack! Catherine little imagined what courage that interruption had taken. Nor did she realize how unheeding he had been as she rolled forth her arguments. (She had just been reading an article in *The North American Review.*)

"But, you know, I have been wanting to speak for..."

"I thought you knew better, too," Cathcrine continued a little sorrowfully, "a person of my ambitious aspirations" (Catherine lived for ambitious aspirations), "isn't going to be happy settling down into a general entertainer and housekeeper for mankind, always sweet and pretty and dainty, standing every evening on the little porch all tumbling over with honeysuckle, dressed in white with a red rose tucked in my belt (that's your ideal, isn't it?) and a hand stretched forth in undulating curves to welcome you. This way." Catherine stood up, balanced herself and nearly fell down. "No, I can't even do it. And then I'm not 'sweet and lovely.' I hate 'sweet and lovely' girls. Why, every girl who hasn't any looks, or any brains, or anything else, is considered 'sweet and lovely.'"

"I never said you were 'sweet and lovely.'"

"Oh! then you consider me horrid and disagreeable, do you? Well, that's flattering. No, I can't marry you. Such a catastrophe has never once entered my head." Catherine grew pensive. "I can't imagine anything more frightful than playing the piano, arranging flowers, and being charming, to eternity." Jack had jumped up from his seat by the piano and stalked over to the window where he stood biting his lips and beating the floor with one foot, gazing out into the black night with an impatiently reflective air. When Catherine finished, he spoke half to himself and half to the night.

"Just what Charlie Dickenson warned me would happen. 'See here, old chap,' he said, 'if you don't want to be the laughing stock of the whole club you'd better steer clear of Catherine Neville. Those college girls are chock full of notions. I suppose she does like you in a way, because you listen to her theories. But it is a ticklish business.

Remember poor Harry Cockran, the trouble he had!' ... I thought she liked me. But I see now that one can't expect anything sensible from them." Catherine did not appear to listen. She was playing a series of changing chords on the piano. But the chords grew louder and louder and gradually passed into the minor key, until at the last word she spun round on the stool.

"Sensible?" she exclaimed. "That depends upon the point of view. I think we are extremely sensible. For we can be reached only through our minds, not through our emotions. Any girl can fall in love. But few have the strength of mind to see that they are needed for loftier careers. We have ideals, aims, purposes."

"Exactly. You long to be strong-minded, to take to platforms, stand up for poor oppressed womankind, and generally make a lot of trouble. Why all the men say that nothing would induce them to marry college girls. They think it's ruination of a nice, pretty, sensible girl to send her to college, and let her head get filled with all sorts of ideas. I tell you it ruins them with the men. But I had rather hoped you were an exception, or at least above the average."

"You men are too exasperating. You inherit from your grandfathers poor, foolish, worn-out ideas that stick in your stubborn, narrow-minded little brains. No amount of eloquence on my part could convince you of anything else. I might talk myself blue in the face, and there you would sit, placid and serene in the error of your judgment. Nothing could change you, except, perhaps, a change of grandfathers. I suppose you consider it woman's place to—bask in your radiance. Well, I sha'n't argue with you. What's the use? I hate a quarrel. Why don't you go? Don't you see that I have had enough of you? Don't you see that I am annoyed with it all?" Catherine was walking impatiently up and down the room, tearing the roses at her belt—his roses—and flinging the petals on the floor. "I hope I shall never see you again." Then, in a lower tone, "(No, I can never love him. I am thoroughly convinced of that.) What are you waiting for? No, I shan't say good-bye. I shouldn't feel it. I am thoroughly miserable. I thought you were such a good friend of mine, too. I can't be polite. I'm tired of being polite when I feel rude. I am tired of hearing all this twaddle about marrying college girls. I think you might have had more tact." Catherine rushed from the room and upstairs.

Jack Livingston heard the door at the top of the stairs shut, not quite gently.

Catherine Neville was a junior at Bryn Mawr. Most people considered her proud because of a certain haughty reserved exterior, but her intimate friends who had pierced the reserve knew her to possess a really genial nature, and on occasions to become quite mellow and entertaining. But it was only with a favoured few that she descended to jocosity. She was conceited, too. There is no doubt about it, but who that ever amounts to anything isn't? at least just a little bit. Perhaps she was spoiled. But if that was the case, it was scarcely her fault, because she was an only child, and had always been pampered and praised and led to consider herself a really remarkable young person. As a small child her mother had looked upon her as a budding genius, and had cherished and retailed to forcedly enthusiastic friends her various idiosyncracies—undoubted signs of genius. But when she grew a little older, and scorned dolls and "*The Five Little Peppers*,"[44] things had gone too far. "A little genius is all very well, but a great deal is so conspicuous," Mrs. Neville used to say. (The Nevilles belonged to a very old Philadelphia family.) The last straw in a long line of disappointments came, however, when Catherine announced her intention of going to college. "A daughter of the Nevilles in college! Preposterous! It is all very well for a girl who has her own living to make. But a Neville!" And Mrs. Neville and Mrs. Neville's friends held up their hands in indignant, old-fashioned horror. Catherine had also indelicate aspirations toward a career. But she kept these to herself until she was safely launched upon her freshman year. Even then her plans were very misty. She thought perhaps she would consent to being considered a second Mrs. Browning, or possibly a George Eliot. It was a dreadful blow to Mr. and Mrs. Neville when Catherine passed all her examinations. Up to that time they had kept themselves happy with the thought that Catherine might fail. Of course Catherine was very clever, but they had always heard that it took a monstrosity to pass the Bryn Mawr entrance examinations. Mr. and Mrs. Neville were especially vexed because their plans had all been upset, and they had formed such delightful ones, too. She was to have a "coming out" tea in November, followed by a series of dinners, culminating in a ball early in January—with a possible wedding at Easter. What more could a girl wish? But Catherine was undoubtedly peculiar. She refused to be trotted out at teas and put through her paces at the Monday even-

---

[44] A children's book series, created by Margaret Sidney from 1881 to 1916.

ing dancing class. She said that dinners bored her, and balls were a frightful nuisance, and she didn't want to be married off. And so it was that Catherine never "came out," but passed into that atmosphere of social depravity and advanced ideas that old-fashioned conventionality has associated with a woman's college.

Is it to be wondered at that Catherine had lost her self-control just a little bit this evening? College with her was a very tender subject. Nevertheless as she stood upstairs with her head near the crack of the slammed door waiting to hear the front door latch, she felt desperately ashamed of herself. But how could she be expected to give up the pet dreams of her youth—all at once and for a man? She didn't like him much, anyway, and she still longed for her career. In fact she quite expected it and such an emergency as falling in love had never once entered her mind. Of course she had seen a great deal of Jack, but he had never been anything to her, at all. Yet he was quite nice, infinitely nicer than the rest of the men. They bored her. The conceited little idiots thought every girl they saw in love with them, and that all they had to do was to sit and be adored. But Jack somehow was different. He had so much more to him. He was so big and fine, so noble look-ing. He had such good-looking shoulders. Somehow she liked to see them around. She might have stood him for his shoulders, at least, until the end of the Christmas vacation. But it did make her furious to hear men run down college girls and say that they didn't want to marry them. Just as if the college girls were pining for them! Men would be much nicer if they didn't consider themselves charmers. "Still it will be frightfully dull now for the last few days at home," Catherine thought as she fixed her hair. She was used to seeing him about. And now no one would ask her to go skating. She didn't want to go skating with any one else. And they used to have such interesting talks togeth-er too! Well, it was all over now. She might as well go to sleep. So she snuggled up in the down comfortable and said she would make her mind a blank. But there was always a little something there, edging her on to the forbidden subject with most annoying insistence. Jack was always mixed up in her thoughts, and she kept wondering if he really cared for her. Of course it was nothing to her. But it is nice to be liked, and somehow it worried Catherine dreadfully to think that per-haps he didn't care for her. "Oh, but he must care or he never would have spoken as he did," Catherine exclaimed out loud. And then, frightened at her own voice, she muffled her head in the bedclothes.

Catherine's thoughts wandered off to her freshman year and that afternoon early in spring when she had received the telegram from her father—

"Mr. Livingston will call at eight o'clock.

"W. D. NEVILLE."

Catherine had read it slowly for the second time and wondered who on earth "Mr. Livingston" was and what she had done that deserved this punishment. She finally decided that Mr. Livingston was a friend of her father's, some nice old gentleman who took an interest in the higher education of women, and wanted to be taken around the college. "Night's a bad time," she reflected, and speculated happily on the chances of $10,000 toward the library building. Nevertheless she did not feel quite comfortable until she was safely at dinner with the doors closed. One never knows what elderly men interested in the higher education of women may do. They are always so intensely interested. He might come out in time for dinner, just for the beneficial experience of seeing how this strange product of the human race eats, and whether or not, as has been said, it lives exclusively on fish. "He is probably of a deeply enquiring nature and will want statistics," Catherine mused. "I must review mine. Let me see. There are sixty-seven 'grads,' one hundred and nine freshmen and——" But, alas! these were all she knew. Well, she could at least explain the "Group System." A complexity of that sort would be something for the old gentleman to gloat over. She knew it quite well now. She had just had some lessons on it from the sophomore next door. And then, of course, there was the seventeen per cent. statistic. How stupid in her to forget that! She had heard it often enough, at least twice a month since she entered. "Yes, that will make a very good beginning," and Catherine sprinkled her beef so vigorously with salt that she was forced to send for a second supply.

Dinner had just reached the salad stage, when the maid whispered to Catherine, in mysterious tones, that there was a gentleman in the hall who wished to see her. "Mr. Livingston!" she gasped, and rushed out. "How fortunate that dinner is almost over! But perhaps the poor man is starving. Oh! but I can't have him in. I'll be hard-hearted. I'll hope that he had a chicken sandwich and a glass of milk at Broad Street Station. But what a strange man for father to send!" Catherine thought as she cordially grasped the hand of a beery object in the dark corner of the hall. "I beg yir pardin, miss, but I'm Jim Maloney, and me wife as does yir laundree is very poor, en has siven childrin en wants to be paid." The man held toward her a soiled, rumpled half sheet of lined paper. "One dollar and twenty-nine cents," Catherine read between the blots, and remarked to herself that there were only five children last week. But supposing there had been twins, she ran singing upstairs and munificently raised the amount to one dollar and thirty cents. "The dollar and a quarter is easy, but four cents is such a difficult amount!" she said, excusing her extravagance, while taking her seat at the dinner table again. "One always has to hunt through all one's coat pockets, stamp boxes, and various trays and receptacles on the bureau, and do at least fifty cents' worth of nervous worry and scurry, perhaps even then not finding the four cents." Catherine was happy again, for she still had forty minutes of liberty, ample time in which mentally to run through a possible con-versation with an inquisitive elderly gentleman and arrange all her ma-terial in paragraphs with a suitable introduction and conclusion. She felt as if she were going to make an address, and had a wild desire to begin. "Esteemed elderly gentleman, it gives me great pleasure to ex-pound to you this evening the—etc." But of course that would never do.

At exactly five minutes after eight Mr. Livingston's card was handed to Catherine. "Elderly and investigating gentlemen are exas-peratingly prompt," she murmured. "He has evidently taken the 7:15 train from the city and has killed time about the campus or been lost for ten minutes," she thought, as she glided downstairs, settling the bow of her ribbon collar primly in front. "Yes, Mr. Livingston," she rehearsed, "the freshman class contains one hundred and seven girls, average age, eighteen; average height, five feet five inches; average weight— Oh, dear me! I've forgotten my average weight, and that was to have led to such interesting discussions of the comparative amount of nutriment in the different preferred foods."

Just at this moment Catherine reached the door of the reception-room, gave her belt a last little twitch straight and walked in. From the least brilliantly lighted corner of the room arose a tall, broad-shouldered man of twenty-five. Poor fellow! He had shrunk there from pursuing pairs of eyes! "Dear me, it isn't the inquisitive, elderly gentleman after all," Catherine pouted disappointedly as she and Mr. Livingston took their seats at the extreme ends of a long sofa. "Now, my plans are all upset." Catherine wanted to say, "Who are you, any-way? Why aren't you inquisitive and elderly? That type is so interest-ing!" But that didn't seem polite, and he looked harmless, so she spoke of the weather, and the walk from the station, the ride out in the train, and the people one sees in Broad Street Station, and hoped that time would unfold the mystery. Just then the top of a head and two eyes rose perpendicularly above the window-sill in front of them, remained stationary for a few seconds, and then sank slowly, followed by a suppressed giggle and the sound of fleeing footsteps. They both saw the eyes, and both being interested in proceedings outdoors, for-got for a moment the absence of conversation.

"Yes, Mr. Livingston," Catherine finally droned forth absent-mindedly. "There are one hundred and seven in the freshman class, average age, eighteen, average height, five feet five inches, average weight, two hundred and eighty pounds, and only seventeen per cent. will marry! At least——"

"How extraordinary!" interrupted Mr. Livingston, while Cathe-rine awoke with a start and wondered if a little fresh air would not be beneficial to both of them. Another pair of eyes arose above the win-dow-sill. There was a second pause and Mr. Livingston said that he thought it would be delightful to look at the grounds. They waited a moment just to satisfy the curiosity of a third pair of eyes and then wandered out on to the campus. It was deliciously balmy, but as it was nine o'clock on a moonless night their horizon was limited. Still by peering industriously they could distinguish a few dark objects that Catherine explained to be trees, and by means of her descriptive pow-ers (she never knew she had any until that night), Mr. Livingston was enabled to enjoy the distant prospect of Rosemont and the rolling hills beyond. When they returned to the reception-room, Catherine felt quite recovered from her little attack of absent-mindedness and hoped that the air had been equally beneficial to her uncommunicative visi-tor. "I have been talking too much," she thought as she watched the careful descent of eyes number four. "Poor Mr. Livingston has not had a chance to enlighten me on the subject of his personal history. I must be silent." A fifth pair of eyes appeared at the window, and the silence was unbroken for such a long time that Catherine in desperation launched forth upon Political Economy theories. (Political Economy and History were her majors, and she always turned to them in times of need.)

And so it continued all evening. Catherine was still ignorant of her visitor's history, but she had counted twenty-seven pairs of eyes. She wondered if Mr. Livingston's and her count agreed. She had counted hers on her fingers, but had a dreadful feeling that she had made a mistake of a hand somewhere and was five too many. Mr. Livingston looked mathematical. She longed to ask him how many he had seen. Finally the witching hour of ten arrived. There was a scampering of footsteps through the hall and a long tolling of Taylor bell. A maid wandered uneasily up and down before the reception-room door. Catherine knew it was time to put the lights out, but somehow said nothing, for she had noticed certain symptoms of uneasiness in her visitor, and felt they were about to culminate in the "good-bye" that had been worrying him since half-past nine. They did culminate, at twenty minutes after ten, when he at length departed. Catherine wondered why men stay two hours and a quarter when they come for a half-hour call. Perhaps they think that they don't appear to be enjoying themselves if they leave before their two hours and a quarter is up. The substance of the letter that Catherine had mailed to her father that night briefly stated would read: "Who on earth is Mr. Livingston? Please restrain him from calling again."

Gradually Catherine returned to the present. She didn't see how Jack could care very much. Then she bounced over on to the cold side of the bed and held her eyes tight shut. Still her thoughts rambled on.

The next day Catherine looked pale and wan. Her mother thought she had better stay in bed and rest because there were only four days left of the vacation and she mustn't go back to college all worn out. But Catherine thought she needed air. The house oppressed her, so she decided to go for a walk in her most becoming clothes. Jack always went to the office between nine and half-past. Perhaps she might meet him. But what could she do if she did meet him? Bow stiffly? That would not be especially satisfactory, but what else could she do? She couldn't appear sorry for what she had said last night. And yet she would like to have him find it out—indirectly. No, she wouldn't go to walk. It wouldn't look well. She would take her mother's advice after all, and go to bed.

Jack in the meantime felt like a culprit. He had spoiled everything by his inane lack of judgment. He ought to have known better. He should at least have remembered the career. It was all up with him now. But he felt sure she liked him. If he had only made a few pretty speeches, complimented her a little and broken the ice gently! He feared he had been a little abrupt. But it wasn't his fault if he couldn't talk. He meant a lot more than the other fellows who have it all at their fingers' ends. But girls never can appreciate fine men. Anything does, if it is only well-dressed. And yet Catherine had really shown a great deal of discretion. In fact she had openly preferred him to the other men. Somehow she had always evinced much pleasure in his conversation. Perhaps it was because he listened to her theories and the other men wouldn't. Oh, but it couldn't have been that! Anyway, he had enjoyed hearing her talk. He couldn't bear the chatter of most girls. Yes, she was a fine girl, always well groomed and a thorough-bred, the kind of girl with whom a man liked to be seen walking down the street. Perhaps she hadn't meant it all. He thought he ought to call again, but he didn't exactly care to go where he wasn't wanted. Still he decided to throw aside his pride and call that evening at the Nevilles, just as if nothing had happened.

But all his hopes were shattered when the maid informed him at the door that Miss Catherine could not see any one that evening. "A polite way of asking me not to call again," thought Livingston, as he hurried off. He was really annoyed now and vowed never to go near the place again. The maid forgot to tell Catherine about the call.

John Livingston had recently been admitted as junior partner into the firm of W. D. Neville & Co. His rise had been rather phenomenal. Five years ago, in the summer time, three weeks after receiving his A. B., he started out bravely to work his way up in the world from the very beginning, and having entered the steel and iron works as an or-dinary labourer, he had come to be a foreman of the shops. It was then that he attracted attention by his remarkable industry and popularity among the workmen, and thus came to Mr. Neville's notice. Mr. Neville at once appreciated his clear business head and knack of getting along well with men and pushed him on, so that he passed from one position of trust to another until he was finally admitted into the firm as a junior partner.

Worldly people might have imagined that Mr. Neville had designs when he sent Jack Livingston out to call on his daughter at Bryn Mawr, and when he encouraged his coming to the Neville house, especially during the holidays. Frequently—two or three times a week—Jack was asked to dine until it became such an expected event that he always stayed to dinner without being asked. But any one who knew the family at all well would laugh at the worldly idea, for Mr. Neville well knew the fruitlessness of forming designs upon Catherine's future. In fact no one realized so well as Mr. Neville that Catherine had no time for anything except her career and that she didn't care for men. All she wanted was peace and a name for herself. Perhaps Mr. Neville was dubious about Catherine's ability to become a Mrs. Browning or a George Eliot. (He was an exceedingly practical man.) "Of course Catherine is exceptionally clever," he used to say. Nevertheless he felt or at least hoped that her mind was well balanced, and doubted the arrival of those expected bursts of genius on which she built so many castles in the air.

During the four days that remained of the Christmas vacation, Jack persistently refused to come to the Neville house to dinner. He was always busy packing or something. This was a bad sign. To be sure Jack was going to Chicago in a week, but every one knows that a man never starts his packing until eleven o'clock on the night before his departure. He goes into the first store he sees on the day of his arrival, buys all the things he has forgotten and never again mentions the subject. Therefore Mr. Neville was a little worried, but he kept quiet and reassured himself by thinking that Jack's shunning the Neville house was merely a phase in an ultimately satisfactory love affair. He did not tell Mrs. Neville his plans or his woes. He knew her too well, and never confided delicate little matters like this to her kindhearted, bungling management. Poor Mrs. Neville! with the best intentions in the world, she always ruined everything.

Catherine, in the meantime, was not at all like herself. She moped, scolded, and was generally irritable and unpleasant. Her mother could not imagine what had happened. Catherine was so changed; she

sat around and looked mysterious and gloomy and absolutely refused
to go anywhere. To be sure she had never been riotous in her pursuit
of pleasure, but still she had always gone about a good deal, and had
really seemed to enjoy things in a characteristically unbending way.
But now all was different. Mrs. Neville was in despair and promptly
jumped to the conclusion that Catherine was suffering from nervous
prostration brought on by overwork at college. Mrs. Neville had always said she would have it, and really there was nothing else that
could make her act so queerly. "Catherine is so energetic," she told
her friends when they came to console. (They all felt sorry for Bessie
Neville. Her daughter was such a disappointment. Their own daugh-
ters all did embroidery in the morning, and went to teas with their
mothers in the afternoon.) "Catherine must be in everything," she
said, "and never is satisfied to do things half-way. No wonder the child
has broken down. I shan't let her go back. No," and she set her
mouth firmly, "health after all is the first thing to consider." Nevertheless their old family physician persuaded her that there was nothing
like work for nervous prostration, so Catherine, in spite of the firmly
set mouth, appeared at college just in time to register. However, she
was loaded down with pills, tonics and strict injunctions to write all
developments of symptoms.

Catherine was glad to get back. She had never spent such a dis-
appointing holiday. Yet though she felt horribly mournful and wandered about with the gloomy, tragic expression of a person with a past,
she hoped she could fight it down, work and forget everything. She
would either have to do that or be wretched always. For she knew Jack
would never come near her again. Of course she did not want to see
him. She was simply annoyed at his neglect. Why, from what her
mother said, it seemed as if Jack had absolutely planned his "good-
bye" call at the house to miss her, and had then apologized as if he
hadn't known. Well, everything had happened for the best. She was
really becoming too much interested in Jack Livingston. But now she
could forget it all, and work and make something out of her life.

With mid-years, a twenty-four page essay, Latin and English private reading and all sorts of unfinished odds and ends of labour, one's
previous misfortunes vanish behind the rapidly accumulating wretchedness of the four weeks after the Christmas vacation. This is the period at Bryn Mawr when one wonders what on earth became of the
first part of the semester, and one firmly resolves this time at least to

keep good resolutions and never again be guilty of such improvident idleness; this is the period when one wakes up on bright, crisp mornings to the wretched realization that an examination is due next day in a subject of which one knows or feels that one knows absolutely nothing; this is the period when, after struggles too painful to describe, one turns up on the fatal morning pallid but resolute, armed with a pen and scraggy blotter and with Tennyson's immortal words "theirs but to do or die," ringing in one's ears; this is the period when after seizing the examination questions one thrills or congeals in proportion to the number of intimate friends, bowing acquaintances or total strangers there enrolled. Nevertheless one survives even the worst, though in a more or less battered condition, and after two weeks punctuated with these periods of violent searching thought and despairing drains on the imagination, one at length emerges into the happy serenity of the middle of February.

So Catherine having passed through the wear and tear of midyears had almost recovered from her attack of nervous prostration. One day she was sitting on the floor in her study chatting happily with some friends. They had finished their chocolate, and the empty cups had been pushed just wherever it was most convenient to put them and most inconvenient for them to be, when Emily Ashurst broke into the general talk with, "By the way, Catherine, I had a letter this morning from a friend of mine in Chicago, which I think will probably interest you. You know Jack Livingston, don't you?" Catherine nodded, and grew a little pinker than usual. "You know, he went to Chicago early in January on business connected with some steel works out there. Well, he was quite popular and taken around a lot and now they say he is engaged to a girl there, a Miss Lyla—oh, bother!—well she is exceedingly pretty—just the sweet, piquant marrying kind that a man adores. They say it was a most romantic affair. Sort of love at first sight. He is perfectly devoted and her friends are delighted with the match. Mr. Livingston has taken them all by storm." But Catherine was not particularly enthusiastic, so the conversation drifted on to basket ball possibilities for the spring. Catherine, however, was not in the least interested in basket ball now, though she was considered one of the most promising forwards. She felt awfully tired, and was secretly relieved when there was a general uprising from the floor and all her guests departed in a flock. Then she was left to her own unhappy thoughts and the concentration of chocolate cups in the one spot that always appealed most strongly to the naturally sympathetic disposition of the maid when she came to straighten up in the morning.

"Jack didn't care at all then," she said, and swallowed a pill. She felt that her nervous prostration was returning, and the pills were the least objectionable of the medicines. "If he had cared he never would have become engaged within six weeks," she sighed. But she didn't see why *she* should care. He was nothing to *her*. But her father would be so disappointed. He was interested in Jack and didn't approve of men under thirty getting married. And then it really was most inconsiderate after the way he had spoken to her. "I suppose I shall have to write and congratulate him. That's a bore! I never know what to say to engaged people, anyway. Yet I should like to write to him, just to show that there is no ill-feeling, and that I am really quite pleased to hear that he has at last persuaded some one to take him. I'll make the letter rather stiff and formal. Yes, I must write. But suppose he isn't engaged after all, wouldn't it seem as if I were forcing myself into a correspondence with him? No, it wouldn't appear well to write, at least, until the engagement was confirmed." Catherine glowed with newly awakened hope. She was glad she had decided not to write, for she dreaded to involve herself in any more awkward predicaments. They were so wearing on the mind.

In the meantime the day was drawing near when Catherine's story must be handed in for *The Lantern*. But nothing seemed to have developed. On several occasions she had sat down, well provided with white receptive sheets of paper, ready to pour out her soul. She had gnawed her pencil and looked bored for half an hour, and then had jumped up and rushed outdoors for some fresh air. Each time she had been expectant and eager to jot down the ideas she thought would crowd into her mind. (One never knows what may happen when one is actually provided with pencil and paper.) But somehow nothing had come, and she really felt now that she was altogether too wretched for ideas.

In desperation she decided to prune and nourish a little love story based on her own affair. It would amuse her, and no one need know that it was not purely imaginary. You can make things so much more real and vivid when drawing from your own feelings and experiences. Of course she would exaggerate a great deal and make it more interesting. And in her story the heroine could write a letter of congratulation to the hero in Chicago, a letter meant to be cold and formal, but into which had crept, in spite of herself, a plaintive, sorrowful strain. (Catherine thought that part quite romantic.) The hero on receipt of the letter could be very much mystified. He was not engaged and had no intentions of becoming engaged, though there had been a rumour. But reading between the lines he should see the heroine's love for him—this part of course could be entirely imaginary—pack his dress-suit case and take the first train for Philadelphia. He should then rush out to Bryn Mawr and throw himself at the heroine's feet, and all would end happily. (Catherine sighed deeply.)

The end, however, presented difficulties, for where should she have the hero throw himself at the heroine's feet? The reception-room was such a public place. (She thought of the pursuing pairs of eyes that hunt one out of the darkest corners of reception-rooms.) Finally she fixed upon the Vaux woods. It was such a picturesque spot, she knew Jack would have liked it. "Yes," she said to herself, "he must restrain his feelings until the heroine has bowed him into a portion of the Vaux woods, where they will be uninterrupted by giggles."

The story was handed in, and toward the end of May made its appearance in the pages of *The Lantern*.

In the meantime Jack Livingston, on the shores of Lake Michigan, was becoming desperately tired of going to dinners and looking out for the Chicago interests of the firm. He wanted to see some one who really cared for him, some one who would ask him out to dinner, even if he did not represent W. D. Neville & Co., of Philadelphia. He wanted to be asked out, fondled and admired a little for himself. Perhaps he was homesick. At any rate he decided to shirk social duties and spend an evening quietly with the Hammersleys. There was such an air of homelikeness and happiness about their evenings. Charlie Hammersley had been an upper classman of his at college, who had married a Bryn Mawr girl a few months before. And now they had a cozy little box just within the margin of respectability of the North End. They were still at dinner when Jack arrived. So he threw himself into an armchair by the library table and reached out for a magazine. The first he threw aside; he was tired of actresses' pictures, and hated novelettes. But something prompted him to investigate the next, though it was unfamiliar. "*The Lantern*, Bryn Mawr," he gasped in pleasant surprise, while he ran his eye eagerly down the table of contents for a certain well-known name. Before long he was buried in Catherine's little love story.

When the Hammersleys came in from the dining-room, they found Jack standing with one arm against the mantelpiece and a far-away expression in his eyes. He started when he saw them with an, "Oh! ... awfully glad to find you in ... You see I've just dropped in to say good-bye before starting for Philadelphia, to-morrow morning."

"Philadelphia?" Mrs. Hammersley asked in surprise. "You're an old fraud. I won't believe a word of it. You know you said you never wanted to see the place again. Besides you sent word by the maid that we mustn't hurry because you had come to spend one of those old-fashioned eight-to-eleven evenings with us. Shall it be whist or hearts to-night? Lyla, you'll make a fourth? ... Let's have hearts to-night. I don't feel strong enough for whist."

"No, really, I can't. You know, I should like it above all things. But I have my trunk to pack and arrangements to make. I'm going rather suddenly. You see I've just decided." Jack wished he was not clutching *The Lantern* so tightly in his left hand.

At Bryn Mawr finals were over and the "'Varsity"[45] had been picked, so that all excitement was now centred in the alumnæ game. After years of success, the undergraduates had got into the way of looking upon this game as a walk-over. (It is hardly the fault of the alumnæ, if one or more years of leisure do not add to their agility!) But now that the alumnæ had the last year's seniors, the champions of the college, to choose from, the under-graduates secretly trembled.

For this reason there was unusual excitement over the game, and the greater part of the college was sitting cross-legged around the bas-

---

[45] The author's use of the apostrophe of omission in the term *'Varsity* denotes that this story was written in an era much closer than ours to the time when *'Varsity* was just beginning to separate itself from the word *University.*

ket ball field cheering excitedly, while a few rushed importantly up and down, flourishing lemons and towels. It was the beginning of the second half, and neither side had scored. The undergraduates felt weak, while the small group of alumnæ at one corner of the field were clutching each other excitedly. Every one was too much interested in the game to notice a tall, broad shouldered man who had just joined the outskirts of the crowd and was anxiously following with his eyes every movement of the 'Varsity's most graceful forward. But two minutes of play remained, the ball seemed rooted in the alumnæ territory and the undergraduates were pale and heaving with suppressed woe, when the alumnæ lost the ball and it passed quickly down the field into the hands of the 'Varsity's tall, graceful forward. For one silent second she aimed, and then amid shrieks of joy the ball spun cleanly into the basket, while, with a little gasp of pain, Catherine Neville, the 'Varsity's pet forward, sank fainting upon the ground. Her ankle was badly sprained. When Catherine recovered consciousness, the tall, broad shouldered man from the outskirts of the crowd, was leaning over her, a most distressed expression in his eyes. In spite of her pain, Catherine gave a little gasp of pleasure. "He does care for me after all," she murmured under her breath. Her eyes grew dim and she felt herself going off again into unconsciousness.

Another summer had passed by and the juniors were now seniors, but one of the most popular members of the class was missing. Catherine Neville was to be married in November. As she said to one of her friends, she was satisfied, and Jack was satisfied, and they didn't see why they should wait. Anyway, Jack was awfully lonely out in Chicago, all by himself, and it was her duty to go out and cheer him up.

Catherine had decided upon her career. She had found her purpose in life.

Harriet Jean Crawford, 1902.

THE APOSTASY OF ANITA FISKE

I

Anita Fiske was no longer wholly absorbed in the student life. This was all she herself understood. Any one else would have seen only generosity on the part of the Fates in the pleasant passing for her of busy days; that is, were it not customary to refer to the interposition of the Fates chiefly on occasions of dire calamity or of some especially flagrant instance of human incompetence or indolence—and indolent or incompetent Anita was not.

The right to be described by very different adjectives would have been granted to her by the most captious critic in her college world. There is a lack of finality in the judgment of this world; even members of it could be brought to agree, if you specifically raised the point, to the truism about the test through the larger issues in the world outside. They could indeed justly claim that their estimate of capability was a very decently fair one; also their estimate of capacity for enjoyment; but, unfortunately for the final value of their opinion, sometimes later on the fortunate possessor of these excellent capabilities and capacities may insist on turning to pursuits calling for another set of capabilities which she does not possess; on the other hand, since she is obviously very young, her capacity for enjoyment may remain as great and yet insist on a change of diet and she remain hungry while trying to satisfy herself with once fancied dainties. Such a double falling away as this from the true faith may even occur before the close of her college days. But—there are some perversions merely temporary of the true and correct inclinations.

This fact might comfort the critic in certain cases, perhaps in that of Anita Fiske, should any of the above considerations be held to apply to her. Her world would certainly have dismissed summarily such foolish speculations. For where, it would say, could you find one more obviously and conspicuously fitted to the grave charm and still, harmonious activity of the student life?

Anita was the daughter of a clergyman who, after years of conscientious if not over-successful care for the spiritual welfare of a country town, was accused of ultra-liberal tendencies and to avoid vain discussion had resigned his pulpit and moved to New York. The family migration had occurred but a few months before Anita entered college; she was a New Yorker in name only,—she avowed this somewhat sadly, for a passionate affection for this city of her adoption was one of the anomalies in her character. So at least her friend Isabel Oakley felt, for Isabel was a born New Yorker, a younger member of the most light-hearted of families. The Student and the Gayety Girl[46] their companions nicknamed the two friends, calling them after characters in a play given two years earlier.

One grey February afternoon Isabel roused Anita who sat looking out with wide eyes on the still winter country.

"Come, you lazy object, you dream too long. Is it of the life history of a root?—a Gothic root, I fear—with due respect to your preference for mould over mere modern earth. I insist upon—well, not snow-balling," as she looked from her goodly height down on the slender figure, "but at least on a race when we have left the proprieties of the village behind."

"Very well—but I scorn your insinuation in regard to roots. Look at this."

She drew her friend down beside her and pushed the yellow curtains more wide apart. The pale light of a winter afternoon fell across long stretches of snow and on burdened trees, bending down heavy branches as though to rest their weight on the firm earth; and sometimes a little mass of feathery snow slipped noiselessly from its uncertain bed and roughened where it fell the smoothness of the white ground.

In a few minutes the two were going down the walk and out through the old entrance between low walls, now mere shapeless mounds in their covering of tangled, snow-laden vines. Anita seemed even more slender, though perhaps a trifle taller, than one would have imagined seeing her crouched on the window-seat. She had quick mouselike movements and walked with sudden little starts as if she feared to lag behind, and from her grey eyes all dreaminess was gone. The other girl moved smoothly and easily with the swinging gait of a strong young animal and held her head high to the cold wind that

---

[46] The musical comedy *The Shop Girl* (opened in London 1894, 546 performances; opened in New York 1895, 72 performances) featured the dancing chorus Gaiety Girls and a plot prominently involving a medical student.

came over the open valley from the hills in the west. Strands of bright hair blew over her forehead and were tossed back as they threatened to blind her quick brown eyes.

On the bridge over the railroad the wind cut sharply. It poured along the black road below, between high banks the whiteness of which was beginning to grow dim in the unequal contest with smoke and cinders. A woolly St. Bernard leaped from a neighbouring garden to greet Isabel as the two hesitated for a moment; when they started again he fell in behind and trudged patiently on, with only an occasional gambol which resulted in much floundering, the snow being deep and his paws at their clumsiest age.

Beyond the last houses of Rosemont village the girls bent to a long, slow hill and, in spite of quickened breath, refreshed themselves after the long silences of the morning and early afternoon, and the ordered speech of the classroom, by wandering remarks, quick question and answer and an admiration for the fretwork of trees against the sky more freely expressed but less interjectional than is perhaps the custom among other more frankly emotional girls.

Their talk instinctively drifted back to the work they cared for, though with avoidance of detail of necessary drudgery or the friction in routine. Truly original work only Anita had; but Isabel's interest in original work was as deep as her own and perhaps more free from the jar of conflicting desires. This interest of hers would have been another cause of perplexity to a self-appointed critic of the two. Isabel was a society girl by birth and tradition, and at college, through the impetus of all her previous associations and also through the adaptability which gained her immediate wide acquaintance, she was confirmed in her destiny—popularity. But, though the instinct for much intercourse with one's kind and the superabundance of animal spirits may close to their possessors the gates within which the still scholar lives, yet even such may truly care for those quiet places and look almost with reverence on the things which there stand first. In this fashion Isabel regarded the work in which Anita was already noteworthy—in their small world—and in which it was possible that she might stand above the rank and file even in the world of research outside, if the promise of these first years should be fulfilled.

The talk turned to an Icelandic saga on which Anita was working.

"Have you tried doing it in verse as that bit was done in an English magazine last winter?" Isabel asked, "or did it ring better in prose—but I am afraid of the excellences of prose. Of course the original I can only respect from afar,—but that German professor's version—what was his name?—had, I know, sacrificed the real spirit to a monumental accuracy. Now please don't tell me you too prefer his version, as you do the Revised,[47] for that same sordid reason."

"Most excellent Churchwoman! you object to change in the Authorized[48] nearly as much as you would to a change in the Prayer Book.[49] But really that piece that came out lately—of the saga, not the Prayer Book,—was quite inaccurate," Anita musingly added. "I am puzzled. I should care immensely about doing the whole thing as you have wanted me to. Bits go well. I confess I have done several when the spirit moved too hard. I could go on now I know." She raised her voice to be heard in a sudden gust. "It was written, or sung rather, to such a tune,—but up in the Seminar room the passion for accuracy falls on me and a sense of pride comes when I detect the accurate Professor Wirthau in an error. I quite despise that piece in English you spoke of. But now, come, I am in the other mood. Let us go into partnership. You have a turn for verse. I supply dry fact and you transform it into poetry. Let a few of your friends work for you and drop from some one committee—or will this have to wait till next year?"

"Next year!" Isabel smiled at her friend. "You are an institution here, Nita, no one would dream of breaking your work off, but mine, such as it is, comes this year to its natural end in an A. B. and next year I shall be disporting myself among—well, not Norse sea kings. My little sister is to come out with me, you know, and as mamma is not strong I believe my superior age and learning are to serve all but the formal needs of a chaperon."

"You a chaperon!" And Anita looked with amusement at her friend.

"I assure you I should make an excellent one. You mistake my character. It is almost portentously tempered with gravity. Will you race me from the church," she looked up at the deserted and lonely

---

[47] The (English) Revised Version of the Protestant Christian Bible, published in parts, 1881-1894. This version was commissioned by the convocation of Canterbury (Church of England) to revise the King James Version to update language.

[48] The Authorized Version, or original King James Version, of the Protestant Christian Bible, first published in 1611 for the Church of England.

[49] The Book of Common Prayer, first published in 1549 (Church of England).

Church of the Good Shepherd they were then passing, "to the other, the cathedral?"—to St. Thomas of Villa Nova, she meant.

"Poor Mr. Clumsy-paws," Anita stopped panting, "he is far behind."

After the tired dog had caught up with them, looking reproachfully, they left behind the bleak church which lifts its golden crosses with uncompromising directness to the winter sky.

Through the fantastic snow twilight an hour later, they climbed the winding hill road to the college. Yellow lights shone steadily in ordered array—a few dark figures passed by somewhere—then a bell rang out suddenly and they hurried in. Yet before turning to the serious duty of preparing for dinner Anita let herself again be caught by her more alert friend idling at the window.

"Another problem, is it? in addition or subtraction?"

"Subtraction," she turned from the cool stars and rushing wind to the staid greeting of books and manuscript, "but what I am subtracting is, perhaps, no such loss after all—an unknown quantity, you see."

II

Anita had just received her father's answer to her letter. Letters are notoriously liable to different interpretations according as one confines oneself to the desires and emotions expressed therein or to those not expressed therein,—not to the uninitiated, that is. Parents are not likely to be the initiated: they have dealt too long in obvious literalness with their children. So, when Anita in her letter laid undue stress on her father's need of her and several other needs classed as domestic, he saw only an overdevelopment of the female conscientiousness in matters household—and a spirit of sacrifice which he duly admired. "Quite heroic, for her heart is set upon staying on at college," the old gentleman had remarked half aloud as he smoothed out her letter.

She read his answer as she sat before a cheerful little fire, a quaint figure in a red and blue flowered kimono. It was the interval between dinner and the time to dress for a college reception. Gay little noises came from the corridors as, by bright coloured screens, soft pillows and stiff potted plants, these were changing from mere means of communication into places of refuge for those who preferred to satisfy their social needs with a lesser degree of illumination and crowding than the large dining-hall, now reception-room, afforded.

Anita fingered her letter. She found it conclusive. She also found herself uncertain as to just the sentiments with which to regard it. His need of her was quite ignored. That annoyed her; but obviously in this she misunderstood him as completely as he had misunderstood her. The letter spoke of the vocation of the scholar and the sacrifice to it of the lesser things. To this she agreed, or thought she did, but had any one seen the grey eyes as they looked fixedly into the fire, he would have seen in these eyes a hunger which was not perhaps wholly for scholarship. Anita had, at the time with full conviction of sincerity, suggested a plan for going on with her work in New York. There were libraries there for the books needed—if one travelled a good many miles. Her father, most wisely and clearly, as she recognized some-what wearily, spoke of the difficulty of concentrating one's mind on serious work among the distractions of a great city. He himself had once dreamed of a scholar's retirement.

She watched a blue flame curl over the edge of an unburned coal and die down again. She well understood this desire and had even felt it herself. A few years before in Oxford, where she had stayed a month during her one trip abroad, she had longed for just such a life. She remembered how, on one of those summer afternoons in the long vacation, she had sat on the coping of a deserted quad and looked across the tall sunlit grass to a flowering white rosebush which clung and climbed over the grey stone tracery, and then had turned back to the worn inscriptions on the wall behind her in memory of those who had worked there many years before. For her the oak stairways up from the cloisters led to anchorites' cells where men worked through endless, still, summer days. She was very young then and only in Oxford during the long vacation. On her return she first saw Bryn Mawr and then she said, with entire conviction, that to be there would be very well. The long low buildings half covered with creepers suggested, as she saw these also deserted and on a summer day, her dream of life at Oxford. Disillusionment, since then, of course there had been. She had objected, more than a healthy girl with steady nerves should object, to the sounds of girlish talk and laughter, to the many mechanical details of college life, and only found the dream again when night had long come down in quietness and she saw the outline of halls and campus trees soft and still in the moonlight, all signs of newness gone and only a few lights here and there to suggest the silent student. Of late she had shrunk less from the rush and gayety of noise, her objection lying now more against a certain crudity in enjoyment which seems unavoidable at some stages—in either sex.

And now as she sat in the bright kimono and watched the little flame curl and die and half heard the sound of gayety outside her door, Oxford was no longer her dream city. The bored dweller in towns who echoes the praise of rural life and poses a martyr to the weariness endured in the city, may smile at her for a foolish maiden, yet true it was that now she longed for nothing more vague and unknown, nothing more romantic and delightful than simply New York. She longed not merely to see it as now occasionally for a few brief days but to live there, to breathe its heavy air, whether that be tainted or pure, to hear the clamour of its streets. To watch it there, would give for her an added charm to the coming spring, to see it as it touches the city square making this fresh and green in a frame of busy walls with patterned beds of daisies and pansies or early blooming crocuses and a springing fountain in the midst. Here every one knew her. She wished the wish most familiar, but for that as urgent, to go day after day down in the streets, one in the changing mass of passers-by, and watch strange faces till the sense of personality was swept away and forgotten. She wished to feel again at night the fascination of a city then most spectacular yet most itself, as one watches it perhaps from a train and, along side streets, one sees in sudden long flashes the streaming white lights. What these lights were, lights of restaurant or theatre or lights of music hall—where she might go or where she might not,—she cared little now, she wanted the picture and the sound. In time she would want more, the dinner, the play,—this, however, was all she now saw in the fire; but of this she wanted her fill.

A voice, she knew it for Isabel's, spoke just outside the door. She would never tell her all these idle wishes, for Isabel had, or at least would soon have, herself the reality of all of them and seemed to hold it lightly. She, Anita, had once spoken with a bit of impatience of some excellent phase of college life and Isabel's eyes had grown troubled as though the light words were almost a sacrilege. How very much mistaken their little world was in its opinion of the two! Anita's lips curled up in a little satirical smile and Isabel entered the room.

"Not ready, Nita? A kimono, however charming, is unfortunately not the recognized costume for social occasions in this benighted land,—except for our fellow-students of Japanese persuasion, so haste you into frills and furbelows."

There was a party like any other,—bright lights, gay dresses, a little music and a Distinguished Person,—only a little more movement, groups of girls drifting about together and watching rather than making a part of it; a party taken, perhaps, not very seriously; one, also, which broke itself up into many little ones, these, in some cases, subdued groups of victims gathered in for the amusement of another person's unfortunate importation,—in other cases, guests discreetly chosen from those not utter strangers to each other; and one heard, here the accents of a southern town, there the soft "thee" of those who, small in number, have yet made their own a city's nickname; a party on the whole not homogeneous, restless and shifting, with a disproportion even greater than usual between the lightness of pale fabrics and the sombreness of men's dress, a disproportion tending, even, it might seem, to social joy—to judge by the greater gayety in purely feminine groups.

On a stiff settee under the broad stairway Anita was established in the midst of a group of Isabel's friends. It was one of the wisely chosen little parties. All included in it belonged, in effect, to one set in the city that counts numberless sets courting recognition and as many more courting the opposite. There was among those around Anita a lady with presence, also a man who had, curiously, refused to be a slave to his bank account and, at forty-five, was causing many misgivings to his friends—and much solid content to himself—through this emancipation. The lady with presence was not his wife, else the emancipation would still have been unaccomplished. There were several strong clear-eyed young men who were still revelling in the untroubled joy of the first years of an independent income; and they took life too seriously to enter quickly into the serfdom which follows after. Now they were preoccupied with buying much pleasant experience in this country and others. A few of them might, in addition to pleasant living, do something worth while, one had already done it, all were rather worth knowing.

Anita's face was a little flushed and she was talking more than usual, though the air of habitual stillness yet clung to her and her hands lay quiet on her lap, half covered by the soft deep ruffles of her blue gown. That she was a student of excellent promise was not known to those about her and Isabel, from long experience, avoided, when within earshot of her, the smallest reference to even the least of her friend's attainments. They did see only a very pretty girl who was talking gayly of all sorts of things in New York with a delight which was charmingly out of place, it seemed to them, among these surroundings; for they could not forget behind the mask of party dress the fact, almost a menacing one to them, of its being a woman's college. As they were New Yorkers by inheritance and much more by education Anita was unconsciously giving them subtle flattery, especially as what she asked about and evidently cared for was not merely the teas and dances uptown but the work and play down among the tall buildings. Isabel sat smiling at Anita's beauty—she gave the word unreservedly that evening—and wondering at her animation among these people who she had feared would bore her friend sadly.

An allusion, a name, suggested a plan for the following winter and they turned to Isabel.

"You are to be with us then?"

"Yes," she answered, "I leave here in a few months." The note of regret was almost evident.

"And Miss Fiske?"

"Ah! she is fortunate," Isabel answered quickly for her. "She has other things to fill her days. No, I refrain from untimely allusions but we all envy her life next year and the year after—for it is all planned, is it not?"

"Yes," Anita replied after a little pause, "I shall only be a few days in New York. I am to be very busy."

The flush died off her face and, as she herself was silent, the talk drifted away from her: when Isabel looked at her next she saw again the quiet face as she knew and liked it best with a gravity which well avoided seriousness,—the eyes a little larger and darker than usual under the bright lights.

Ellen Rose Giles, '96

A DIPLOMATIC CRUSADE

Sunday after Mid-Years. A grey biting February afternoon, with a promise of snow in the eager air, was darkening over the deserted campus. The examinations, which had finally dragged their slow length to an end on Friday, seemed to have left a peculiar haze in the mental atmosphere; for throughout the college, whence all who could possibly do so had departed for a brief rest, there was a subdued and slightly melancholy air, as though no one had yet realized that another four months must elapse before the agony of having her knowledge investigated would again rack mind and body.

Eleanor Mertoun, deep in the comfort of her cushioned window-seat, alternately mused on the contrast between her busy Thursday self and her lazy Sunday self, and wished for the return of her room-mate, who was spending the Saturday and Sunday in Philadelphia. It was certainly the time and place in which to enjoy the retrospect of work done. The red glow of a quiet little coal fire in the grate mingled pleasantly with the fading cold light from without, and lit up warmly the dark green walls of the study, and its polished floor. An antique oval mirror in a dull old gilt frame dimly gave back the double of a graceful sword fern which spread its long fronds over the end of a well-filled bookcase below. Eleanor, being in a contemplative mood, stared hard at the fern and reflected that *it* toiled not and was very beautiful. Before she could go on to the philosophic consequences of her meditation, the door was swung open vigorously, and in came a tall figure in hat and ulster.

"Why, it's Marjorie Daw herself," exclaimed Eleanor, springing up to greet the longed-for roommate. "I thought you weren't coming back till to-morrow? You're just in time to save me from acute melancholia, but I can't believe you had any premonition of that!"

"I'm *gefrohren*[50]—give me a cup of hot tea, for the love of—Me, and then I'll tell you," answered Marjorie Conyngham, as she threw

---

[50] German, "frozen."

off hat and coat, sat down on the rug by the hearth, and held out both hands towards the fire.

Eleanor dashed out to fill the kettle, and soon had a steaming cup and a "jammed" cracker ready for Marjorie. Then she put a "Busy" sign on the outside of the door to guard against too attentive friends on borrowing bent, sat down beside the newcomer, clasped her hands around her knees, and commanded, "Go on."

"I had an unusual and severe attack of piety that prevented me from cutting Pol. Econ. in the morning. It was brought on, I think, by the idea of having to copy six pages of lecture notes on the social state of the indigent Indians."

Eleanor interrupted her. "Oh, I don't in the least care what brought you, now that you're here. I meant, I want to know all about the Atkinsons, what you did and said,—and how many times you upset your glass at table."

Marjorie passed over this insulting thrust, and irrelevantly re- marked: "Isn't it a pleasant thought that exam. time is over, and so Betty Hall no longer goes down the corridor warbling 'Earth is my resting place, Heaven is my home,' or 'I'm a pilgrim and I'm a stranger, I can tarry, I can tarry but a night'?"

Eleanor laughed at the remembrance. "It is, surely. Poor old Bet- ty! Doesn't she suffer more from the fear of being flunked out than any upper-classman you ever saw?—and she makes elaborate prepara- tions for going home at every exam. time. But come back from this digression and stick to the manuscript. Marge, conversationally you're a tramp!"

"About the Atkinsons? They're very well, thank you.—Oh, don't break my head with the tongs and I will be good! I have a lovely tale to tell you, really, Eleanor. I met a man——"

"Impossible!" interjected Eleanor.

"Who's digressing now?" demanded Marjorie.

A meek small voice from the gathering darkness said "Little El- lie," and then Marjorie went on; "a man whom you know quite well in the general if not in the particular—a handsome, well-groomed, mid- dle-aged man with iron grey hair, serenest confidence in his own judgment and estimate of things, and—here you may perceive the rub, Lee—unconquerable prejudice against the essentially modern wom- an—in the abstract."

"Ah!" breathed Eleanor, scenting the battle from afar.

"In the concrete, I confess, she shows him to be 'not impregnable as a bulwark of archaism,' as Dr. Phillips would say." Marjorie was smiling at the fire, which was only half lighting the corner of the dim study. "Eleanor, from the moment that I first heard that man speak and open fire on the kind of thing the modern girl is going to become, I marked him for my prey. Oh! it was lovely," laughed she suddenly, rocking back and forth in an ecstasy of delighted amusement, "it was lovely to see the mighty fall."

"Do tell me how it happened! What did you use on the poor man?" asked the eager Eleanor.

"It wasn't force, hardly even force of argument. He did not know I was a Bryn Mawrtyr at first, and so he was led into jesting with me just as he would have with any mere society girl who was ready for badinage. When he fathomed my real character his face was an entertaining spectacle—a mixture of regret, astonishment, and—well,—annoyance, such as one is not always privileged to see. I saw he was preparing for driving me out of college by hot argument, so I got out my strategic tools and turned the conversation.

"You know we have threshed this all out before so many times, and raged to each other about the quarter of the population who take us, without looking, for mannish boarding-school girls, as empty-headed as the women of ten centuries ago, but more silly because we pretend to be what we are not; and about the other quarter, who look upon us as grinds and blue-stockings, star-gazers impossible and undesirable to touch with a pole of any length! This man had a smattering of both those ideas, and was—is—bringing up his daughter on principles impossible to classify. He told me all about his plans for her before I quite got the conversation turned from the explosive topic, and I feel sure the poor child will find herself an anachronism in ten years.

"I knew it would shock him fearfully if I talked politics; but besides being anxious to shake him up a bit, I really wanted to do battle with Mr. Atkinson (as usual) about England's policy in South Africa. And so I launched on that perilous undertaking, making as gallant a defence of Oom Paul and all Boerdom as I knew how. To my huge delight, the man (his name is Ballantyne) had to acknowledge that he disagreed with Mr. Atkinson and agreed with me! Point No. 1.

"Just then Teddy Atkinson began talking music. You know he is very enthusiastic—goes to the Symphony concerts, all the operas, and that sort of thing. He asked about the Glee Club at college, and wanted to know if I were still Leading-Grand-High-Soprano-in-Alt, or something equally foolish. You should have seen Mr. Ballantyne's face—looked as if he thought music and political science mutually exclusive terms. I plunged in at once and talked 'technical' all I knew how. Don't think me a horrid *poseuse*, Lee, though I was playing to the gallery in a way. I didn't pretend to very much more than I knew, and besides it was all a part of my deep-laid plot for bringing down that man."

"You! posing!" was Eleanor's sole comment. "Go on."

"You see my scheme? To let no subject of conversation escape; whether it was anything Mr. Ballantyne had ever heard of or not makes no difference. The point was to convince him, as thoroughly as was possible in one short evening, that I, in the character of college woman, was neither a bit of thistle-down nor a fearful prig. The next thing was—oh yes!—domestic affairs. Mrs. Atkinson, without knowing it, helped me immensely there. She began the topic, and though my knowledge of it was so theoretical that if I had been an angel I should have feared to tread on that subject, I rushed in. Fortunately, I had gathered enough information from running the house last summer while mother was away to talk without utter nonsense. I told them about the cook who said, when I went down and criticised some of the products of her skill: 'It's yersilf I'll set on the stove if yez do be afther interferin' in *my* bisnis!' And I thought Mr. Ballantyne's amusement rather excessive for one who disapproved so heartily of me and my college. Perhaps he took it as a welcome proof that I couldn't manage cooks. It proved a good transition anyway; for Mr. Atkinson was reminded of one of his delicious stories, which made me think of some lovely tales we heard from Betty Hall and the frivolous-minded Dorothy at the fudge party after Philosophy exam. on Friday; and then of course the Ballantyne had one to tell, so that the table cheered up markedly. I could see now that he began to think me amusing if peculiar, and I gained an inch whenever I could.

"After that we went on talking about all sorts of things, for Teddy Atkinson couldn't have played better into my hands if he had been an accomplice, and suggested the most diverse known subjects. College settlement was closely followed by wireless telegraphy, yacht races, and golf, especially at the Merion Cricket Club; and though I had to be wary of terms sometimes when it came to the second and third, I didn't back down once—not once. Then Mr. Ballantyne and I had a bit of a talk together, in which I tried to introduce 'a current of new and fresh ideas' into his mind, and gently remove some others already there. I think his capitulation would have come very soon if he had stayed longer, for when he rose to go he said that he did not know whether he would find it best for his daughter to go to Bryn Mawr, but he hoped she would prove as many-sided as he had found a college woman might be. Wasn't that worth working hard for?"

Eleanor, leaning over and spanning Marjorie's forehead with her hands, murmured "Undue cerebral enlargement——"

"Lee—you idiot!" cried Marjorie, "do you imagine for one moment that I would have spent a laborious, uncomfortable, self-conscious evening to make any living person like me on my own account? I didn't care what Mr. Ballantyne thought of *me*—I wanted to make him like the college girl in me, and show him how utterly he was mistaken in his baseless notions of what college makes a woman."

Marjorie was roused now, and in earnest, and the light carelessness was gone out of her manner. Her wide grey eyes, Eleanor could see by the fire-glow, were shining with an eager light and her usually pale cheeks were richly flushed. She rose from the hearth rug, and leaning with one arm along the mantel, forcefully punctuated her words by tapping her finger-tips upon it.

"Lee," she said in her clear voice, "we're at a sort of crisis now, I think—not the same ring that there was, well, about twenty years ago, when the question was, shall women go to college? That has been answered, and the answer is, yes, because they *will*. But now there are quantities of people, just like Mr. Ballantyne who think the fact that women will do it adds a most unfortunate complexity to modern life; and the burden of proof that college is the right thing for us lies with us. I don't mean that we are to claim more for it than it can do, or pretend to more than we have, but to be so broad-spirited and alert and interested in everything, that we shall simply convince these people that college training is the best thing that ever happened to women—especially Bryn Mawr training. *I'm* going on a crusade against all infidels of the genus Ballantyne. Will you go along?"

Eleanor took Marjorie's outstretched hand and laid her other on her roommate's shoulder. "Of course I will, Marge, as far as I can. But I'm not capable like you, and can't do half——"

"Yes you are—yes you can," was Marjorie's confused answer. And she went on dilating upon Eleanor's being "a shark at Major English" and many other delightful things, until that embarrassed young woman sought a brief respite in a tour of investigation for the match box, an article of furniture which seemed bent upon disproving the theory of the conservation of matter, for it was rarely to be found. This evening, by some strange chance, it was discovered on the bookcase, and Eleanor seized it with alacrity. Just then it was useful to her as a diversion rather than as a light-producing agent, but she struck a match from it, lighted a candle, and handed it to Marjorie, saying, "There, take that and go to your room. Your hair looks frumpish with so much excitement, and if you don't hurry to do it you will be locked out, for the bell rang ages ago. Think what it would be to miss Sunday evening supper!"

Marjorie vanished behind the portière and continued her flow of flattery, which Eleanor by singing "Ancient of Days," rendered inaudible. Then they discovered they had but one minute in which to get to the dining-room, and fled down the corridor with other late stragglers to reach the goal of their desires before a dark and cruel hand should bar them thence.

Marjorie's cause could have found no better champion, no one more fitted to illustrate her theory of the influence of college training on women, than herself. She was one of those healthy inspiring people, becoming ever more numerous especially among college women, who do everything well, if not all things equally well; and who show how invaluable is the discipline which has given them largeness of view and a certain ready grasp of affairs often lacking in those who have missed the same training. She saw life steadily, this senior of twenty-two, (though she could not as yet see it whole) and therefore she was neither scatter-brained nor priggish. The ideals of balance, proportion, symmetry, self-control, had been growing clear and attractive to her all her four years, but they had crystallized in her thought only in the last.

As she had said to Eleanor, they had "threshed it all out before," and the occasion of their so doing had been this:

Marjorie, aspirant for athletic as well as academic and social success, practiced basket-ball at every opportunity; and after winning her class numerals by playing as substitute in a match game in junior year, was in a fair way to make the senior team. One rainy November afternoon, Marjorie, in default of an outdoor game, was throwing and catching ball in the gymnasium with the senior captain and a junior.

As she ran across the floor after a muffed ball (which brought down upon her much reviling by the captain) she noticed a spellbound freshman standing in the doorway—a freshman whom she knew slightly. It was a friend's friend whom Marjorie had been asked, as upper classmen are every year, to "look up"; and when she had done so had found a rather repressive young person, of serious-minded intent to study, and do nothing else. When Marjorie saw her "little freshman friend," as Eleanor called Marian Coale, with her eyes glued to the white numerals on Marjorie's dark basket-ball suit, she nodded to her, and later, when they all stopped playing, walked off with Marian, as she had to stop at Radnor Hall, where the latter lived.

"I didn't know you played basket-ball," the freshman had said suddenly.

"Too awkward?" asked Marjorie with a quizzical expression in her shining grey eyes. "Or a weakling—which?"

The freshman was visibly embarrassed. "I didn't mean that, you know," she stammered, "but I didn't think you belonged to the set that cares for—that sort of thing." She was gaining confidence now, and went on somewhat loftily, "It's rather a waste of time, don't you think? just as so many teas and plays and things of that sort are. I think we come here to work." She glanced at the senior stealthily as she delivered this startling opinion, and was a little annoyed to find her smiling broadly.

"Of course that's what we come here for," cried Marjorie, "but you'll find that you do your work about forty times better if you do something else as well." Then she had spent a few moments expounding her views to the serious-minded freshman, leaving her slightly bewildered and semi-convinced that there were some things she had not fathomed in her month of college life.

Marjorie had met before several girls who had gone through and out of college with similar aims; but she had not found the type a prevailing one, for, happily, at Bryn Mawr there exists not only strong adherence to the high intellectual standard, but likewise a healthy tendency towards general culture and breadth of interests. Marian Coale was one of that minority whose ideal is only knowledge, not wisdom. She bade fair to become a bookworm—of high order, it is true, but yet a bookworm, and a bookworm, as a factor in life, is, by common consent, less desirable, admirable, and useful than a woman.

Marjorie's attack upon her theories, coming as it did from so well recognized a student, was from the right quarter, and was well-timed to give the freshman a new outlook even in her first year. "I hope I didn't inculcate too much frivolity," said Marjorie as she was telling Eleanor of this *rencontre*.[51] "I tried to make her see that I did not mean quite being a Jack-at-all-trades, and missing the kernel of college by running every organization to the exclusion of lectures. But I toiled to show her that the opposite sort of mistake is nearly as fatal in the end. I am hopeful of having her try to make the Glee Club, and perhaps write for the 'Philistine'! If she turns out a swan in the literary line shan't I deserve a vote of thanks from the editorial board?"

"You won't get it unless you warn Caroline Brandes beforehand that 'M. C.' signed to any copy means Marian Coale as author and Marge Conyngham as inspirer and motive power," answered Eleanor in her dry unsmiling way. "What started you ramping like a lion against the greasy grinds, Marjorie Daw?"

"I shouldn't have done it before the end of senior year anyway, Lee, and probably not then if I had not come across so very inviting a grind as Marian. You see she is one of the Coales of Hampstead, who are friends of the Dorsets, and so I have heard of her very often. There is so much possibility for all sorts of fine things in her that I can't bear to see her shutting everything but one out of her life, even though that one be books. Be a good friend to her, Lee, by showing her that even the president of Self-Government and the next European Fellow——"

Eleanor's strong hand shut off Marjorie's speech, for not even by her roommate would she suffer her chances for carrying off this, the highest of undergraduate honours, to be discussed. She now informed Marjorie that if she wished to go on telling about her schemes for Relieving Socially Indigent Freshmen, she (Lee) would listen with joy; but approaches to any other topic would be instantly punished. And so Marjorie returned to her tale.

It was *à propos* of this episode that Marjorie and Eleanor had "threshed it all out," as the former said in discussing Mr. Ballantyne; and during the process had been half-formed in Marjorie's mind the idea which, though growing slowly during the long winter, reached its full maturity only later when warmed and ripened by that gentleman's

---

[51] French, "encounter."

noble rage against women's colleges. Marjorie saw that her crusade must be carried on both within college and beyond its peaceful campus. "You see, Eleanor," she said, "all the Marian Coales in the freshman class (I am afraid it is too late to work with hardened upperclassmen) ought to be given a good broad point of view on the question of what they are to get out of college: and *then* all the Ballantynes in the world outside are to be convinced that such a point of view exists—is more common than they think. What gives me most hope about the second half of the work is that the Ballantynes of the world are nearly always people who have met no college women, or few and unfortunate specimens of the race."

With a strong sense of the need of instructing people of the Coale and the Ballantyne type in the way they should go, Marjorie began her last Semester in college. That, however, was only one of a number of conflicting ideas behind that broad, white brow of hers. For a senior's last Semester, by reason of her desire to do her remaining work at least well enough to merit that coveted title of Bachelor of Arts, and her intention to spend more time than she has hitherto spent with the soon-scattered members of the dear old class, (tramping with them about the country to the Gulph, Valley Forge, and the Red Rose Inn, or gathering congenial spirits about the hospitable chafing-dish)—by reason of all this, a senior's second Semester is a time of great physical activity and some confusion of mind. Marjorie worked indefatigably at her beloved political science, took part enthusiastically in Sheridan's *Critic* when that delightful drama was given for the benefit of the College Settlement Chapter, and when basket-ball training began in mid-March, cheerfully forswore all sweet things and "eating between meals," that she might, when the time came for the inter-class match games, help to win the silver lantern for the class of __.

And as she worked and played her thoughts were never far from the crusade she and Eleanor had undertaken. They told no one of their efforts, but they were often amused by the way in which their friends unconsciously forwarded their plans. Carroll Mayo, dubbed by Marjorie the "Versatile Virginian," was a gallant supporter; for though her record for scholarship was not so high even as Marjorie's, it was high enough not to be despised by the respecters of intellect only, in estimating her total strength. As for her power in other directions, Carroll was considered by this somewhat remarkable group of seniors the best "all round" girl among them. If Marjorie chanced to have a guest of the Ballantyne type, (and it must be confessed that she laid traps for many such by inviting them to dine or have afternoon tea) she generally contrived that Carroll should sit on one side of him or her, and by her unconscious charm help Marjorie banish the prejudice that was waiting to be justified.

Then there were Betty Hall and Anne Aldridge, both of whom were excellent though unconscious abettors of Marjorie and Lee. Betty, in spite of the self-distrust that put her into a very real agony of apprehension whenever examinations stared her in the face, and caused her to announce beforehand that in a few short days she would be "flunked out," was no mean student; and ever since freshman days of Minor Latin had done clever work in the classics. She was likewise a good actor of what she called "heavy female parts," and the owner of a fund of most delightful stories.

And Anne? Everybody knew Anne. Underclassmen gazed upon her with awe and rapture—for was she not captain of the senior basketball team, whom as juniors she had led to the championship? Merry, kindly, black-eyed, sweet-tempered, saucy, loyal, unassuming Anne Aldridge, overflowing with infectious humour, and having a good word for every one—never was any one so justly popular as she. And to describe her yet further with a wild flight of far-fetched metaphor, she was one of the brightest jewels in the crown of the biology professor!

Less considerable than the help given the two crusaders by these three was that which Marjorie and Eleanor received from another unwitting senior—Kate Murray. Kate, if she had not been thrown with such girls as Marjorie, Eleanor, and her own roommate, Dorothy Van Dyke, might have turned out pure grind; but the constant contact with the good friends had bred in her a wholesome sense of the value of a well-rounded college experience. Now, in senior year, although she had at times to be forcibly dragged from work by the frivolous Dorothy, she was heard to deliver herself spontaneously of the opinion that people ought to play daily,—afternoon tea with the six, after a long tramp or basket-ball being preferred as the form that play was to take. And so when outside influence was used to make Kate take her own advice, she was an admirable example to the delinquent freshman Coale.

That clever young person whom Marjorie had found so problematical, was now, by the end of the second Semester, working herself out to a satisfactory solution. The slight change which had already, under the energetic training of Marjorie, taken place in her was re-marked by many who had known her in her freshest freshman days, even though they did not know of the influence that had wrought it. She was more alert, more sympathetic than she had been when first the senior started her upon a course not laid down in the college pro-gram; but not being of an introspective nature, she was hardly con-scious of the utter difference between her former and her present points of view.

Her attitude towards the question of the next European Fellow, (that annual earthquake whose rumblings so agitate the entire college with increasing violence until the shock of the final announcement rends it) was a delightful index to Marjorie of her own success in cru-sading, and of what she considered Marian's improved mental condi-tion resulting therefrom. They talked it over, as do any two Bryn Mawr girls who are together for more than five minutes at this period of the year; and Marian, somewhat diffidently because she was a freshman talking of seniors, said she very much hoped that Carroll Mayo would be the choice of the Faculty. Why? Oh, because she was the sort of person the college might for every reason be proud to have represent it at a foreign university.

Didn't she think other people were as promising candidates? Marjorie had inquired. Oh, yes, but personally she wanted to see a girl as charming and as "all-round" as Carroll win. She thought Eleanor Mertoun another great person for the honour,—supposed Kate Mur-ray had a show, but she wasn't very enthusiastic about *her.*

In the meantime, the senior class, with the best possible right, was in a state of ferment that was not to be relieved save by the knowledge of which one of them was chosen for such well-nigh crushing honour. As March advanced, all other topics of conversation at breakfast, lunch, and dinner, during long walks, or strolls about the campus on the way to lectures, or from the athletic field, were relegated to the forgotten corners of the mental attic; and "who do *you* think will have the fellowship?" was the incessant question.

When the bulletin boards at last displayed the announcement that all the students were requested to come to chapel on Tuesday morning, March 20th, like a leaping prairie fire spread the news that the European Fellow's name was to be made public. At once discus-sion waxed the more violent, that every one might say all she thought before the need for speculation in regard to the chosen one should be past. Monday afternoon, when the final Faculty meeting for deciding the matter was in progress, was spent by the senior class in a state of restlessness that kept them vibrating in a distracted manner between that portion of the campus immediately under the windows of the President's office (as though forsooth any information could trickle, like a welcome stream, down to the thirsty ones below) and the rooms of different members of the class who were so fortunate as to live facing that august building where the fate of several people was being decided. Pembroke East, being nearest Taylor was the favourite place for these indoor gatherings, and Marjorie's and Eleanor's study, which faced the President's office windows, was filled with a constantly changing crowd of eager seniors. In the course of the afternoon, practically every one in the class was suggested; for human nature, in such cases, does not thoroughly like being surprised, and there was abroad a hardly culpable longing to be able to say, "I told you so," in case some dark horse should prove the winner. When the Faculty meeting was over, they knew would come, in some mysterious manner, the official notice from the Secretary of the Faculty to the chosen candidate. Then, in accordance with a wise provision which prevents the spontaneous combustion of the new-made fellow, she might tell one of her friends. And every one longed to be sharer in the secret that was to be kept over-night.

As it happens every year, so too when the class of __ were seniors, the efforts at discovering the recipient of the Faculty note failed utterly, and all but two seniors were therefore ignorant of the long-desired name when the morning came on which the public announcement was to be made. Speculation was rife, and breakfast, contrary to its usual sleepy moroseness, was nearly as animated and "discussive" (Marjorie's word) as dinner was prone to be.

At last Taylor bell begins to ring for chapel, and hardly has the first stroke melted into the clanging monotone of the succeeding ones when on all sides is displayed an unwonted eagerness for attending divine service (not compulsory). From every hall flow long lines of students, the black gowns of the more eager ones streaming straight out behind them in the fresh March wind, like Alice's hair when the Red Queen ran with her "faster! faster!" Followed by the slower comers, they hurry into Taylor, up the staircase and into the chapel. There they scatter to the excited though somewhat subdued groups that occupy the sections set apart by unwritten law for different classes. In the middle front writhes the senior class, forgetful of its usual stony impassiveness in the face of anxiety. They are excited, for is it not one of themselves that has been chosen? They are supported on the left by the loyal juniors, who, because they have known the Fellow (whoever she may be) three years, longer than any other class in college, are in turn justly thrilled. The right flank is held by the devoted sophomore class, excited because those from among whom the Fellow comes were once their champions, when in freshman year they needed such. And behind the choir, which is the rearguard of the seniors, sit the freshmen, excited because they have never before come within hailing distance of the honour.

The clock is anxiously watched as the hands approach, oh! so slowly, towards 8:45. Every probable, nay possible, candidate is being pierced to the soul from all sides with glances compared to which a hawk's would be careless and cursory. Now and again the wave of whispering and laughter rises suddenly, until some conscience-pricked proctor silences the throng. It begins again—a low bubbling noise that is alive with anxious, suppressed excitement, and that threatens to engulf the decorous Chapel in the rise of its un-religious tide.

The nervous twisting about to survey the crowd, the buzz of talk, the ripple of laughter, cease suddenly. Then as the President and the College Preacher, in their academic robes, enter the two upper doors and ascend the platform, the mass rises, and led by the choir breaks into a vigorous processional hymn. Then very quiet is the room while the words of the strong King David are read, and it is only when the last sentence of the prayer brings the students upright that the excitement breaks forth again.

Across the rustle of readjustment, subduing it momentarily as a great wind flattens the waves for an instant only to toss them the more wildly, comes the voice of the President.

"Before we come to speak of the purpose for which we are gathered here this morning," she begins, her smile expressing perfect appreciation of the suspense that racks her audience, "I should like to make some announcements of general interest to the students." The strained attention of her hearers all over the Chapel breaks in hardly audible catches of the breath. Those unheard announcements give time for further speculation as to the candidate. Marjorie is eagerly leaning forward, too impatient-looking for one who knows the Thing—

so it can't be Eleanor, decide the sagest critics. Kate Murray is abnormally flushed, Carroll correspondingly pale. It must be Carroll—she looks so subdued—so unexcited.

Those announcements are over. The President unfolds an innocent-looking bit of paper. The honour list of ten, from whom the Fellow has been chosen, is read. "Is it she?" is the tacit question of the crowd at each name. Then——

"The decision has been difficult," says the President impressively. "After long and earnest discussion the Faculty has nominated to the Board of Trustees, as European Fellow for the coming year——"

A pause. The weighted silence seems to stifle one.

"Eleanor Whitcomb Mertoun!"

A roar shatters the air—or is it the roof?—a shout of generous gladness mingled with the hearty clamour of hand and heel. The pent-up eagerness to know is changed into the longing to honour the chosen candidate, and it bursts forth and swirls tumultuously about Eleanor like the Fundy tide. It rises, falls, rises again, twenty feet at a leap.

Marjorie is meantime pounding Eleanor's knee, and exclaiming to every one within reach, "I knew it! I knew it!" as though some especial credit were due her for having been told the secret. Kate Murray, on the other side, was dragging Eleanor down by the neck, as if she would unseat from its firm base the head whose market value had risen 100% in five minutes.

Decorum returns for a moment when the President dismisses the students with the request that they sing the college hymn; and they sing it as can only those that have felt the "gracious inspiration" of our "Mistress and Mother." When it is over, there is a rush for Lee Mertoun from all sides, for it is *de rigueur* to shake the new Fellow's hand very nearly to the maiming of that revered member. For ten minutes she clasps hands, hardly recognizing their owners in the press; and then gradually, as the bell rings for first lectures, the crowd melts out of the chapel.

As Lee, Marjorie, Kate, and Carroll left the room Marjorie ran her arm through that of the warm and red recipient of blushing honours and facing her quickly about, pointed tragically with her pen at the almost deserted confusion of chairs helplessly awry.

"There, woman," she said, "a picture of that might with great plausibility be labelled 'Charleston after the Earthquake.' That is all your fault, and it is what you have got to live up to."

Eleanor laughed. "If that were all!" she said.

"You are right—there is more," retorted Marjorie, putting her own construction upon Eleanor's words. "You have to live this thing down as well as live up to it. And that means you will have to work hard to convince the infidels that you are still in the crusade, and that you stand for something besides the midnight oil. Now if you have yourself well in hand after all this agitation, let's go to Latin." So the four seniors wended their way through the small groups that were still "talking it over," Marjorie declaring that she simply must cut her own lecture and go with Lee to Major Latin, in order to see how to treat a Fellow.

As they passed into Room E closing the door behind them with the peculiarly irritating, undecided rattle that particular door always gives, suspended animation woke again in the lingering underclassmen, who had ceased their talk to gaze after the person who had suddenly become a Personage in the college world. A knot of freshmen talked in low tones.

"Marian Coale is embittered for life because Marjorie didn't get it," suggested one teasingly.

"I'm not," protested the literal-minded accused. "Marjorie doesn't deserve it——"

"Tut, tut, how disloyal!" murmured the tease.

"—so far as scholarship is concerned," she finished.

"What else would you base the choice upon?" was the astonished inquiry from another.

"That is the first thing to consider, of course; but it is not all." And Marian waxed eloquent upon the subject of the ideal European Fellow.

"Who told you all this?" asked she of the insatiable desire to annoy, when Marian paused. "You didn't have it with you when you came to college."

Marian's dark face reddened. "I am learning a few things in college," was the slow answer. "One is to value something beside pure intellect, and to estimate people at more than the amount of grey matter they happen to possess."

This was quite true. Marian's face-about was a matter of great astonishment to the few who had known her at all well when she entered. Most of them traced the change to her friendship with Marjorie, but no one, least of all Marian herself, suspected that design on the part of the senior had brought it about.

As to Marjorie, she hardly believed in the transformation of the freshman, and kept furtively watching her convert for some signs of flagging energy. But watch as she might she never saw in Marian any indications of departure from the way into which she had been drawn. As the spring advanced, and one was greeted upon going out of doors with the faint, exhilarating scent of new-sprung grass, and the sight of a green patch, like the broadcast promise of the prodigal summer, here and there on the brown campus, Marjorie began to feel that the first part of the "crusade" she had placed before herself that February day had been carried out.

The second part, which concerned the extra-college world of men and women she had in the meantime not neglected. Here, her efforts, though not confined to Mr. Ballantyne, were yet centred in him. She dated her spring, as do most Bryn Mawrtyrs, by the changes in field and tree, but in this particular year she counted time also by her progress with the "genus Ballantyne," and especially with him from whom it took its name. In the time of cherry blossoms, when the black old trunks flung over them a white splendour woven by the wind and the sun, she had broken through the outer wall of prejudice that had been so weakened by her first attack. When the wind began to whirl from the apple-trees the full-blown petals, she felt that she was actually gaining ground, and faster than she had hoped; and when finally the daisies whitened the country-side, Marjorie received proof of complete triumph.

This pleasant reward for the labour of a Semester came to Marjorie one Saturday afternoon in the latter half of May. The days had been warm and, as the work piled up in its inevitable way towards the end of the year, wearisome also. Dorothy Van Dyke, to celebrate the passing of the week, persuaded Kate Murray that they two should give a "Ball" to the other five under the big cherry-tree by Pembroke West. So it came about that lemonade flowed freely there that afternoon, and every one of the seven friends returning from a shopping expedition in town, from work, or what not, was welcomed to rugs, cushions and the cool clink of ice under the hospitable boughs. Marjorie was there, of course, helping every one in her own particularly helpful way. It was restful, sitting there in the golden-green afternoon shadows, while the breath of the lilacs drifted along to them with the lazy air. The beauty of it all silenced the little group more than once, and their love for campus and halls rose breast-high—throat-high, and choked them oddly as they thought of going away.

Dear grey, ivy-clad halls! curtained in April with rich, tender green that is pierced to the heart with glorious sunlight, and that undulates, rippling, in the sweet spring wind; reddened by your vines that burn, lit by the sunset, in October; standing bare, proudly silent when the shouting north wind whirls the white snow about you; roofed with silver when the high moon dapples the grey road with the soft dim shadows of your trees; stately but never cold, always beautiful and beloved; if you but set upon your children as they go forth from you (groping their way because their eyes are clouded) your hallmarks of strong intellect, high honour, broad sympathy, and quick insight—who of all *Almæ Matres* may more truly rejoice in her noble race than Bryn Mawr?

A mood of contemplation could not but soon pass with such a group. The irrepressible Dorothy shattered it now.

"Here's a man coming up the walk," she announced. "Does he belong to any of you? Daughter is with him."

Every one turned to see if he "belonged" to her, and Marjorie seized Lee's arm as she recognized the stately figure.

"Mr. Ballantyne—and Louise. What do you think that means, Lee?"

"Suppose you go to find out," suggested Eleanor. "He probably wants to see you at all events." And Marjorie went.

When she came back half an hour later, after showing the delighted father and daughter as much about college as was possible at that unpropitious time of day, her face was glowing with pleasure.

"Marge," called Dorothy, as she came running across the grass from where she had been speeding the parting guests, "we've decided to cut dinner and stay out here until it's time for the Glee Club to sing on the steps."

"Jolly," answered Marjorie, "who cares for dinner anyway?" She dropped down beside Eleanor and seized her firmly by the shoulder.

"Lee Mertoun, Mr. Ballantyne brought Louise out to see her future Alma Mater. She goes to Miss Stevens's school next fall for the last two years of prep. work—then here to college. *Was denkst du?*[52]

---

52 German, "What do you think?"

Eleanor clapped her hands delightedly. "Good work, Marge! I knew it would come about. Why, at this rate there won't be any of the genus left in the city of Philadelphia—not an infidel to crusade on——"

Betty Hall's voice broke across the stream of congratulation. "Of course, Carroll, I wouldn't mention it to her, but I think it shows just a *little* lack of breeding to discuss something we know nothing about!"

The laugh that followed this expansive hint was joined in by Marjorie and Lee.

"Do tell them about the crusade, Marjorie. It is time now, I think, especially as you have met the enemy and made him yours, poetically speaking. You don't know how I have been burdened by this ghastly secret!"

And while the sun sank and the shadows melted into the one deepening shadow we call twilight, and the circling bats flickered against the sky, Marjorie told of the problem that had presented itself to her that winter, and of her plans and efforts for its solution.

"Of course," she finished, "I don't mean to have it take all my time. There are other things more important, and besides it is not the sort of thing that can be done by constant conscious effort. But it seems to me so very well worth while to convince people at large of the value of college training, that I am willing to go out of my way sometimes to do it. And if we *are* going to do it, we have got to take care that we are broad and sympathetic, and not merely 'cold, learned, dehumanized'——"

By senior year one's friends never let one's statements go unchallenged. Kate Murray as might have been expected, now took up the case for a hypothetical defendant.

"I don't agree with you at all, Marjorie. That's a one-sided way of looking at the matter. You leave out of account, absolutely, the point of view of the people who devote their lives to one particular side of intellectual work, and accomplish the greatest masterpieces of the world. Specialization is the only thing that brings about great results in many cases; and where would be the great works that are above the horrible level of mediocrity, if your doctrine of—of—universal versatility (stop giggling. I'm not trying to be poetic or funny either) were accepted by everybody?"

"See here, Kate," broke in Carroll, "it's you that are getting one-sided now. I see what Marjorie is after and I think she is quite right.

Getting bloodless and thin-lipped *is* one of the dangers of the college woman."

Anne Aldridge's quick voice answered Carroll.

"That's all very well for the world at large, Carroll, but I think Kate has made a very good point in bringing up the case of the great minds of the world. I believe that genius is 'an unlimited capacity for hard work' in more cases than you think. Now if people who have power of that sort should let themselves be turned aside by a desire to be open to impressions from all sides, the world would certainly be the loser by it. I haven't genius even of the hard work description, and so I shall never deny myself the pleasure of as much of your society as I can get, merely to go on pegging away at the regeneration of the pharynx of the earthworm! But if anybody has the power of doing something really great, for the world's sake, don't preach versatility to that person. There are few enough of us that can add to the sum of knowledge."

"That's a part of what I mean, Anne," struck in Marjorie eagerly. "There are few of us that can do that, but there are quantities of people who will never be able to do more than grind, and who yet abstract themselves from the world of actual life as though they were hermit geniuses. I say they have no right to do it, and that they owe as much to their fellows as to their own brains. Don't you see that the existence of such people among us is what gives people like Mr. Ballantyne their opportunity to misjudge the college woman? I've thought a good deal about both sides of this, and I think I have good grounds for carrying on what Lee and I have called, rather as a joke, our crusade. Please don't misunderstand me to mean that the women of really great intellectual power are to let their remarkable work be interfered with by turning that power aside to every little thing."

"So far as we ourselves are concerned," said Kate, "I think we may agree with you, Marjorie; for probably none of us is a genius except our European Fellow—of course she is. And so if we may be allowed to let alone all those bearing the marks of genius, we may join the crusade too. I am willing anyway to help in the attack on the large and flourishing Ballantyne species, and convince it that not all college women consist solely of massive intellect."

"And I too," said Anne.

"So am I," came from each of the others.

"Good children," said Marjorie gaily, as she threw an arm across the shoulders of Anne and of Kate, on either side of her. It was all she said but her satisfaction was deep.

Silence fell among them as it will when good friends sit together. A late robin-song floated over to them from the apple-trees. The evening star, like a sanctuary lamp, swung above the dying altar-fire of the sunset. The cool, nameless fragrance of a spring night filled the air. There under the old cherry-tree sat the seven with no word, until at last the silence was broken by snatches of melody, vague talking, and the laughter from strolling groups. Then, drawn back from their dreaming, they rose and went away to join the singing on the senior steps.

Edith Campbell Crane, 1900.

www.ingramcontent.com/pod-product-compliance
Lightning Source LLC
Chambersburg PA
CBHW030344180626
46812CB00007B/2747